Dealing with Disputes and Conflict

Dealing with Disputes and Conflict: A Self-Help Tool-Kit for Resolving Arguments in Everyday Life offers accessible and practical strategies and solutions to guide untrained mediators and readers on effective ways to resolve disputes and conflict, across a wide range of dispute contexts. Drawing together psychological and social scientific theories, the author offers clear guidance for managing conflict in everyday life, ranging from experiences at work, with the community or at home.

This book defines mediation practice, its key principles, and how it is structured and implemented, and offers practical strategies based on key theories, including Transactional Analysis. Tony Whatling draws on his extensive experience as a professional mediator, consultant, trainer and author, to create this valuable practical guide. Including a toolbox outlining core skills and strategies applied by trained practitioners, the book covers important elements in conflict resolution, such as apology, reconciliation, the importance of listening and concentration, and what to try when disputants do not respond. Case studies from various contexts are featured, giving readers the tools they need when faced with disputes relating to situations such as divorce and workplace disagreements.

Exploring the building blocks of dispute management through an engaging and clear tone, this text is ideal for mediators, dispute resolution specialists, volunteers, community leaders, medical staff and anyone embarking on a career in mediation, as well as individuals hoping to resolve conflict in their own lives.

Tony Whatling has a professional background in childcare, adult mental health, family therapy, team management and has ten years of experience as Head of the Social Work Education Department at Cambridge University. He has over 30 years of experience as a mediator, professional practice consultant and trainer, and has trained hundreds of mediators in family, community, health care complaints, victim-offender and workplace mediation contexts. A founder member of the UK College of Mediators, he has published two books on mediation practice and over 40 professional journal articles.

Dealing with Disputes and Conflict

A Self-Help Tool-Kit for Resolving Arguments in Everyday Life

Tony Whatling

LONDON AND NEW YORK

Cover image: Copyright of © Getty Images

First published 2023
by Routledge
4 Park Square, Milton Park, Abingdon, Oxon OX14 4RN

and by Routledge
605 Third Avenue, New York, NY 10158

Routledge is an imprint of the Taylor & Francis Group, an informa business

© 2023 Tony Whatling

British Library Cataloguing-in-Publication Data
A catalogue record for this book is available from the British Library

Library of Congress Cataloging-in-Publication Data
Names: Whatling, Tony, 1939- author.
Title: Dealing with disputes and conflict : a self-help tool-kit for resolving arguments in everyday life / Tony Whatling.
Description: First Edition. | New York, NY : Routledge, 2023. | Includes bibliographical references and index. | Summary: "Dealing with Disputes and Conflict: A Self-Help Tool-Kit for Resolving Arguments in Everyday Life offers accessible and practical strategies and solutions to guide untrained mediators and readers on effective ways to resolve disputes and conflict, across a wide range of dispute contexts. Drawing together psychological and social scientific theories, the author offers clear guidance for managing conflict in everyday life, ranging from experiences at work, with the community or at home"-- Provided by publisher.
Identifiers: LCCN 2022024037 (print) | LCCN 2022024038 (ebook) | ISBN 9781032328409 (paperback) | ISBN 9781032328461 (hardback) | ISBN 9781003317005 (ebook)
Subjects: LCSH: Conflict management. | Self-help techniques.
Classification: LCC HM1126 .W5294 2023 (print) | LCC HM1126 (ebook) | DDC 303.6/9--dc23/eng/20220726
LC record available at https://lccn.loc.gov/2022024037
LC ebook record available at https://lccn.loc.gov/2022024038

ISBN: 978-1-032-32846-1 (hbk)
ISBN: 978-1-032-32840-9 (pbk)
ISBN: 978-1-003-31700-5 (ebk)

DOI: 10.4324/9781003317005

Typeset in Times NR MT Pro
by KnowledgeWorks Global Ltd.

Contents

Summary of chapters

Chapter 1. The book starts by defining mediation practice, its key principles and how it is structured and implemented. These ideas are drawn from mainstream professional dispute resolution theories, knowledge and practice. They are offered simply as a reference point and framework that can hopefully be readily available to anyone wanting to help themselves or others resolve disputes – without necessarily having to undertake any formal training – in line with the fundamental beliefs listed above.

Chapter 2. Briefly explores and summarises a selection of the very many theories of disputes resolution, with a particular focus on practice.

Chapter 3. Explores one particular theory on everyday interpersonal communication – Transactional Analysis – and its application to practice.

Chapter 4. Provides a list of the known attributes of effective mediators and invites readers to self-assess themselves on a rating scale, in terms of existing strengths and further development goals.

Chapter 5. Introduces the core skills and strategies – often referred to as the toolbox – that are used by trained practitioners. These are explored in significant detail, together with examples of potential applications.

Chapter 6. Focuses on the skill of listening in more detail and demonstrates how good listening is at the heart of all effective communication, across all everyday activities ranging from home, communities, family and successful work and business life.

Chapter 7. Provides a more extensive look at skills and strategies.

Chapter 8. Introduces some of the less familiar elements such as apology and reconciliation, and what to try when disputants do not respond to the process.

Chapter 9. Explores some particular contemporary issues such as dealing with social media communication conflicts – particularly the use of Email and texting – with ideas on how to manage them constructively.

Chapter 10. Includes some potentially useful ideas and concepts that may not have been particularly covered in the main text but could usefully be reflected on by the reader.

Chapter 11. Covers some important cautionary 'health warnings' to bear in mind such as safe practice, managing high conflict, unintended consequences and conflicts of interest.

Chapter 12. Explores the extent to which trained practitioners manage to use their knowledge and skills in managing disputes in their personal life.

Chapter 13. Provides some illuminative case examples from different dispute contexts, which demonstrate the text content in action.

Chapter 14. An overview of the book's main theories and ideas, and the conclusions the author draws from them.

Acknowledgements

For Carolyn and our sons Steve and Stuart for being who and how they are. Also for our grandson Tony, who continues to amaze, amuse and charm us all, and will doubtless continue to do so. Special thanks too to my many clients over some 50 years, who taught me so much about what life was like for them, what they needed from me that helped and what else I could do differently. Thanks also to my many trainees and supervisees worldwide, who made it very clear what sort of books they needed and wanted me to write for them. Finally, my special thanks to the editorial team at Routledge for their very early belief in, and commitment to, what I was trying to do with this book, and who then worked so hard to help bring it to publication.

Synopsis

How to resolve disputes and conflict in the family, at work and with neighbours, before involving professionals or resorting to legal action and Courts.

This book has been written specifically for untrained mediators involved in disputes in their everyday life and work contexts. It will also be of interest to a wide range of professionals working in other contexts, for example, managers; human resource staff; faith groups; local authority employees and managers; social care staff; schools; counsellors; therapists; NHS staff etc. Some mediator colleagues are even predicting that it could be of interest to trained and experienced dispute resolution professionals. Anecdotal evidence from recent consultancy involvement shows that two of the country's largest membership unions are struggling to deal with serious levels of staff disciplinary and grievance procedures. There has been a particularly high increase over recent years, linked to social media communication, emails and texting. Managers and Human Resource department staff report feeling ill-trained or qualified to cope with such disputes and the significant increases in costly disciplinary tribunals. It may also be of interest for team-building activities in the workplace. It should be understood that it will not provide a short-cut route to qualifying as a professional mediator. That process involves lengthy training processes, ongoing practice supervision, detailed competence assessment and registration with a national professional regulatory body, such as the College of Mediators. Nevertheless, it may well be useful as a 'taster' for anyone considering future training for a career in professional dispute resolution.

It is also interesting to note, that from over ten years of involvement as a trainer with non-Western cultural and faith groups – throughout South East Asia, East Africa and the Middle East – the author learned that certain cultural groups often have very different expectations of mediators. As a generalisation, Western individualist cultures, such as the US and UK, prefer trained qualified practitioners, who are not known to them personally. Conversely, non-Western communitarian and collectivist cultures, particularly from the more close-knit traditionalist groups, prefer to seek help from personally acquainted community elders and faith leaders. Alongside such differences there may well also be expectations of a more conciliatory style and, unlike Western styles, perhaps even some giving of advice for settlements by such dignitaries – whether or not such advice was in line with either sides settlement expectations. Such differences are historically rooted in longstanding and very traditional non-Western cultural dispute settlements, through non-legal natural social justice systems.

The term used for an untrained mediator throughout this text is 'lay mediator' (LM). Historically, that term has tended to be assumed to mean a person who is not a member of the clergy. However, dictionaries also commonly now describe it as a person who is not trained, qualified or experienced in a particular subject or activity. It has been difficult to find a more appropriate label for the potential reader for whom this book is intended.

Foreword

As the value of mediation to resolve many different types of disputes becomes increasingly recognised so too does the need for mediators who can adapt their skills to a wide variety of situations. This does not just require professionals to be more flexible: it means that people without any formal training in mediation need a firm grasp of what the role involves and how to use it. This is the important gap that Tony Whatling's new book is designed to fill, and it does so with his customary combination of insight into what really matters in mediation coupled with his ability to make accessible some subtle skills.

Tony is perhaps uniquely qualified to speak to those whom he describes as 'lay mediators' – 'those who are not trained, qualified or experienced in a particular activity or subject' – whose jobs in schools, health and social services, local authorities and private companies require them to deal with the myriad of disputes that can cost employers time and money by undermining trust and corroding relationships. He brings to this 'Self-help Tool-kit' three particular qualities which will make it invaluable to his intended readers and practitioners everywhere.

First, Tony brings over 50 years of experience working with individuals and groups in many different contexts and cultures, and this is reflected in a markedly non-doctrinaire approach to mediation: he knows that every single dispute is different and therefore every intervention by a mediator needs to be individually designed and managed if it is to be successful. Secondly, his approach recognises that most people are good at solving problems and repairing relationships because they already do it, so his focus is to build on these everyday skills, such as listening, summarising and responding empathically, and add to them some of the key ideas, knowledge, principles and 'technical' skills that professional mediators bring to their work. Thirdly, Tony avoids the theoretical rabbit holes down which some texts designed for professional mediators can too easily disappear. So you will not find here any arcane conjectures about the causes of conflict, negotiation or models of mediation beloved of academics or the more legally-minded: Tony is the practitioner's practitioner, who uses down-to-earth language, realistic examples and clearly described methods to distil a lifetime's experience into key learning points.

Do not, however, mistake clarity and concision for lack of depth: there are lessons in this book for experienced mediators as well as for those who find themselves in this role. His observations on the use of apology, for example, and on the value of reflective practice, are both pertinent and significant for all of us.

Finally, it is a privilege to be asked to introduce a book by someone so widely admired and respected in the mediation field who has already done so much to broaden and extend the practice of mediation.

Andrew Floyer Acland
Mediator, trainer and author

Introduction

What inspired this book? This book is predicated on two fundamental long-held beliefs and values by the author about people. These beliefs are based on over 50 years of practice experience, with roots in the social sciences, including psychology and sociology; social work; counselling; individual and family therapy; mediation practice; training and consultation. The first belief is that the majority of people are very good at everyday problem solving, in family, social and work-life. The second of these key assumptions is that most people also already know very well how to use many of the core skills required for mediation, for example, good listening, summarising and responding empathically. It should be acknowledged that such qualities and attributes are often latent in the minds and awareness of would-be dispute resolvers and a potential LM. If indeed, both of these assumptions are accepted as fair and realistic, then it would seem reasonable to posit them as a potential hypothesis. Conjoining the two suggests that many people in their everyday home, life and work activities are regularly helping themselves, and others deal with disputes and conflict. In this case, another reason for publishing this book emerges, that of helping people with some ideas, knowledge, skills and ethical principles, commonly associated with – but not exclusive to – professional dispute resolution. These assumed qualities, along with others, are also the focus of dispute resolution training, primarily to highlight their importance for effective and skilful professional practice. In conclusion, it is these key everyday 'people attributes' and assumptions that are at the root of this book. There are other what can be called 'technical' skills that mediation practitioners need to learn and understand, that would not be expected of an LM. For example, depending on the practitioner's working context, legal and financial matters, couple relationship dynamics, child development, workplace disciplinary proceedings and tribunals etc. Nevertheless, this book will concentrate on dispute resolution skills and strategies that are readily understandable and practised by an LM. The text will also limit in-depth mediation theories, for example, causes of conflict, negotiation strategies, loss and grief and a range of mediation models. There is an abundance of that information available elsewhere, primarily targeted at professional practitioners. However, it will end with a list of useful further reading texts that readers may find interesting and helpful if inspired to follow up on any particular topics. The text also aims to avoid professional language or jargon and, as far as possible, to use everyday language, such as is promoted by the 'Plain English Society'.

Finally, the learning outcome goals in this text are not assumed to be easy to implement in any situation, particularly where the helper is close to, or directly involved in the dispute – so common difficulties and resistances will be explored in detail – together with advice on various strategies for the effective management of such issues.

1 Defining Mediation, Its Fundamental Principles, Styles and Typical Stages of the Process

It may help to start by exploring some very common definitions and principles of mediation from the trained professional perspective.

Mediation is commonly described as a process in which an impartial third person assists those involved in a conflict, to communicate effectively with one another, and reach their own agreed and informed decisions concerning some, or all, of the issues in dispute. Here, we see immediately the term 'impartial third person', which potentially challenges the notion of a lay mediator (LM) mediating with those close to or directly involved with disputants. However, once that difference between professional and lay mediation is acknowledged, it arguably does not invalidate the essential thesis of this book. Note too, the important principle regarding the right of participants to determine their outcome settlements according to their joint principles of fairness. Fairness has always been an interesting concept in dispute resolution, though in general, it receives relatively little debate. For example, in legal proceedings, a judge, in announcing a settlement, may well declare that it is a 'fair judgement' for all parties. However, since it is very likely to be a compromise, compared to what each disputant wished for, all may come away complaining that it is an unfair judgement. From this example, we can postulate that ultimately in reality, the only people who can determine what is a fair settlement are the disputants themselves, and, hence, it must be preferable for them to work together to arrive at a settlement. This may also be a good moment to reflect on a dynamic that is often working in favour and advantage of the practitioner. Particularly with the more protracted and acrimonious conflicts, disputants are often really wanting an end to the fighting and a return to more peaceful and productive times. In such cases, it is not that a settlement is not wished for but it is more a question of how and on what terms. Despite presenting 'conflict saturated' histories, help in such circumstances from a demonstrably impartial practitioner may paradoxically be welcomed by all involved.

Mediation is a staged process

Mediators generally work to a defined staged process. In other words, mediation is not an event as such but a process, or journey, that starts somewhere,

DOI: 10.4324/9781003317005-1

proceeds through certain identifiable steps and concludes somewhere. For trainee and novice practitioners it usually comes as a great relief to know that there is this structure to depend on. It works as something of a 'sat-nav' in keeping track of where they are at any point in the discussions and agenda, whether it is still appropriate to be there, and if not, how to return or proceed to a different place. This can be nicely paraphrased as, if you don't know where you are going, you may end up somewhere else. Writers from different dispute contexts will describe different stages of the process and range in number from 5 to 12 or more. In reality, the greater the number, usually, simply means that the core stages have been broken down into sub-stages. For example, in family mediation, though not exclusively, it has generally evolved as a five-stage process summarised as follows:

1. Assessing the suitability of mediation through solo meetings.
2. The first joint session. Defining and clarifying the issues – equivalent of a meeting agenda.
3. Exploring each agenda issue in more detail.
4. Developing options for the future.
5. Securing agreement and plans for future.

At its simplest, it is fair to say that, as with most third party helping professions ranging from counselling and therapy to mediation, the general framework or process of intervention involves certain identifiable common elements. Each professional group will define these elements and stages in their particular terms and the number of stages. Typically, however, these elements will include finding out what has happened to cause the clients to seek help, (the story); what effect this is having on their daily life and well-being; what those involved have tried to do to resolve difficulties thus far; who else is involved and affected by or affecting the situation; what the clients' hopes and options are for beneficial future change; who will need to do what to bring about their change goals; and, finally, the what, how, who, where and when details of achieving the action plan.

Voluntary participation

Participation in mediation must always be voluntary. Participants should enter mediation of their own free will and, having done so, they and indeed the mediator(s) are free to withdraw at any time.

Neutrality

Mediators must at all times remain neutral as to the outcome of mediation. Over the time, in the development of professional mediation practice, the term 'neutral' has been replaced by 'impartial', since complete neutrality is arguably a near impossible state of mind. Again, these principles may become problematic for the LM working with people known to them, and who may be either directly or indirectly involved in a dispute. At best, impartiality may be genuinely aspirational for the LM, depending firstly on their relational proximity to the dispute, and secondly on the trust afforded to them by other disputants. Should this prove to be impossible, then it should be disclosed to those involved and attempts at mediation by an LM end. Indeed this is an accepted 'Code of Practice' embodied in professional practice.

Confidentiality

Within the professional dispute resolution arena, confidentiality is a crucial ethical principle designed to ensure maximum trust between clients and practitioners. There are certain exceptions, for example, related to the discovery of criminal activities, money laundering and risk of harm, as in the cases of domestic and child abuse. In the application of this to lay mediation, it would be wise to raise it during any initial assessment discussions regarding the suitability, particularly where there may be any line management involved between LM and disputant. In other words, to what extent is confidentiality desirable and achievable, and who in particular should be involved in any such arrangement as included or excluded. Either way, such aspirations will stand or fall by mutual trust and respect.

Privilege

Whilst unlikely to be relevant to the LM it is included, since it may be referred to by others at some stage. Essentially, at its simplest, the legal privilege protects participants involved in mediation dispute resolution and their associated conversation details, from being disclosed in or used as evidence in any subsequent legal proceedings without the consent of both parties.

Procedural flexibility

This principle encourages the application of a variety of procedural approaches to resolving disputes. In other words, it challenges the notion of 'one size fits all' or 'off the peg' styles and encourages a 'bespoke' approach to all disputes and conflicts. Experienced practitioners soon learn that most disputes in all contexts tend to revolve around a range of very familiar stories and examples. Nevertheless, it should never be forgotten that for the people involved, it almost certainly feels unique to them and hence needs to be given the qualities of listening and associated skills it deserves. In other words, each process flows from early exploratory conversations, to determine who else is involved and affected, and may need to be involved, where meetings will be held and for how long they will last etc.

Finally, this section presents a summary of the overall values and ethical framework of mediation which is usefully described by one writer as the values of mediation exemplify a fundamental ethic of respect – for the parties' perceptions, meanings and values, for their autonomy and for their capacity to make choices through the exercise of critical reflection and the awareness of alternatives. These values are seen to be essential if the mediator is to have proper regard for the right of the parties, whatever the difficulties, to be the architects of their own agreements and if *party control* is to have any meaning (Roberts, 2014, p. 65). This quotation needs to underpin everything this book is attempting to cover, albeit from lay readers' potential, for engagement in disputes and conflict. Just as with the world of professional training, qualifying, competence assessment and accreditation, the LM too should avoid acting in ways that are inconsistent with such fundamental values and ethics.

Reflective reading

In the last year or so the phrase 'reflective practice' has found its way into the language of professional mediation. Quite simply, it means that apart from regular conversations with a practice supervisor, it is also important for practitioners to regularly self-reflect on how their practice is developing. This can be a general overall review of various aspects of their practice, its ups and downs and, especially, with meetings that were particularly challenging, and what might be tried differently in future. Throughout the training and novice stages, mediators are encouraged to keep a 'practice log' that records such analysis. That log can then be shared with trainers and their supervisor as well as providing potential evidence when applying for competence assessment. At the highest level of practice standards, total competence and, highest of all, what some regard as 'artistry', these are not understood to be final end arrival points but as sequential lifelong developmental processes. On the basis of such ideas, the following chapters will provide the opportunity for the reader to develop self-evaluative 'reflective reading' abilities. For example, with the above text, the extent to which the definition and principle of fairness fits with their initial interest in possibly assuming the role of the LM. How far the stages of the process offer reassurance, in terms of having a clear structure and also how, from experience, that compares with effective chairing of meetings. Finally, how far the ethical principles feel appropriate, reassuring and achievable, in the context of the sorts of disputes a potential LM may consider taking on in family, neighbourhood or workplace contexts?

---

2 Some Common Theories Summarised

Whilst the book will not cover more than one specific theory for application, it may help to summarise some that have evolved over the years as mediation has developed, so as to give some background foundation awareness. The field of theory in mediation is succinctly summarised as, *Mediation* has been richly theorized since the beginning of the twentieth century and a distinguished body of knowledge exists as an autonomous theoretical understanding... this resource is distinct from the academic literature that also informs the broader study of *conflict* and *dispute resolution* – derived from anthropology, sociology, political science, social psychology, international, relations, socio-legal studies, peace studies, systems theory etc. (Roberts, 2014, p. 172). Given the substantial range of theoretical schools, potentially most useful to readers are probably those linked to practice application, in particular those often referred to as 'models', or styles of practice. General styles, or methodological approaches, cover a range that can be understood as connected to practitioners' assumptions about disputants' abilities to resolve their conflicts. The scale can range from one end, light touch modest third-party help, to the more active giving of advice at the other.

For the first group, practitioners would be offering what is often referred to as a 'facilitative' approach. This style emphasises, re-empowering and perhaps at times mentoring disputants to mobilise their capacity for problem-solving – much as the assumptions that underpin this book. At the next level is what is often referred to as 'evaluative or normative' styles of intervention. Here the focus is on informing people – often from a legal perspective — about what normally happens in cases such as theirs in terms of outcome settlements. The third style is referred to as 'directive mediation' and is often underpinned by evaluative assumptions. Essentially, people are advised as to how they should settle, sometimes underpinned by explicit reference to what a court would impose. There are time and potential cost resource implications here, with the facilitative style commonly taking longer than the latter option. Other writers have formulated models that are grounded in the disputant's competence and mediation as an educative, learning process, from which participants may be better able to resolve other disputes in the future. Examples of such, worthy of further study

DOI: 10.4324/9781003317005-2

include: The Promise of Mediation. Responding to Conflict Through Empowerment and Recognition (Bush and Folger, 1994) – commonly referred to as 'transformative mediation'. Narrative Mediation. A New Approach to Conflict Resolution (Winslade and Monk, 2001). Therapeutic Family Mediation. Helping Families Resolve Conflict (Irving and Benjamin, 2002). Anecdotal evidence from discussions with both Folger and Winslade makes it clear that, not surprisingly, there tends to be a strong level of belief in their model of practice. Alongside that conviction is a strong view that it must be used as the 'whole model and nothing but the whole model', without exception. Equally from experience – whilst some practitioners adopt the whole model – there is a sense that such expectations of many UK practitioners, suggests they are less 'culturally' attuned to such exclusivity, and frequently find that an eclectic pick and mix works best for them, according to the specific behaviours and responses of the disputants.

Reflective reading

To what extent do the different models and styles listed connect with your own values about people and how they solve problems in everyday life? Similarly, how far does the range of options, from facilitative to directive suit your own natural style inclinations, for example, being helped to think through problem solving in a facilitative and empowering style, compared to being told the solution by others? Finally, how far does the idea of the LM practice demonstrating an educative model with potential for resolving similar disputes in the future sound to be a useful additional benefit?

---

3 One Particular Interpersonal Communication Theory for LM Practice

Transactional analysis

TA is a theory of interpersonal communication based on the analysis of sequential 'transactions' between people. Potentially a rather complex theory, when explored in full detail, it can be usefully simplified for its potential application to mediation practice. The theory proposes that at any moment in time, in communication with others, we adopt one of three, what are known as 'ego states', or styles of communication. Practitioners vary in the extent to which they are either aware of, or subscribe to, the value of TA and its application to practice. As with a variety of theories, in particular of psychology, human behaviour and therapies, they tend to be what can be described as 'knowledge not for use'. In other words, they are useful in helping us understand why people behave in certain ways but are not generally regarded as appropriate to being explained to disputants as might be appropriate in a therapeutic encounter. The aforementioned ego states are described as (1) our 'Critical parent state' (sometimes called 'controlling parent'), (2) our 'Adult ego state', and (3) our 'Child ego state'. The states are commonly represented in vertical diagrams as:

$$P \qquad P$$
$$A >>>> A$$
$$C \qquad C$$

The use of capitals indicates that they are a theoretical state of behaving, not a person, and the use of two lists indicates two people in communion. Such ego states are developed throughout childhood and beyond, and it is important to understand that they are not chronological or age-related. In other words, a child can have a well-formed 'critical parent' ego state by as young as three years of age. Hence children can often be heard scolding their dolls for being naughty and doing things they should not be doing. 'Should' is an important keyword here, since the clue that someone is in their critical or controlling parent ego state, is the commonality of their use of 'should', 'ought' or 'should not' 'ought not', to be doing. Typical indicators of someone being in their child ego state are statements such as 'it's not fair'; 'I'm too old to be treated like this'. In contrast to the two

DOI: 10.4324/9781003317005-3

potentially negative and value-laden terms, the adult ego state is what is known as 'value-free'. In other words, when in our adult ego state, we are at our best for problem-solving, and our language is 'uncontaminated' by the negative connotations of the other two. The general principle is that when communications are working well, a response to what is known as a 'stimulus', that is, a comment from one person to another, (see the >>>> in the diagram), will ideally attract a compatible Adult<<<<Adult ego state response. However, a reply from what is known as a 'crossed transaction' – imaging the arrows in the diagram running diagonally back to the first person, for example, from the parent or child states – and may well cause a relationship problem. A workplace example could be where someone might, from their adult ego state ask, has anyone seen the Watts Company file, the response to which, possibly by a manager, from their critical parent state may be — if you took more time and care to file things carefully, you would know where it is. Such a critical response might, in turn, be followed up by a child ego state crossed transaction such as that's just not fair, you know I am way overloaded with work for my pay grade level, and nobody is ever likely to be at their best with such a heavy workload. By contrast, a better adult state response to the crossed response from the manager might have been, that sounds like we need to find time to sit down and talk about my job description, workload pressures and how that could be improved, but in the meantime, the customer is waiting for me to call back urgently, and there is a big contract involved here. There are many more complex levels of analysis involved in TA than are possible to explore here, including, for example, the 'positive critical parent' where there is a genuine concern for safety risks to themselves or others being taken by the other person. Equally, the child state may include positive sub-states such as the 'creative child' – for example akin to what happens between colleagues when suggesting they take time out to 'play around' with some ideas, often called 'brainstorming' or 'blue-sky thinking'. Here, the clue to the creative child state is in the use of the words 'play around'. What is most important for the LM to understand here, is that regardless of any 'crossed transactional' responses, they should stay firmly in the adult-adult ego state. Anecdotal evidence from practice suggests that the longer we can stay in adult, the harder it is for the other person to continue crossing the communications. That may not happen the first time but it most often does get there eventually. For further reading on this theory, see Eric Byrne, 2016 Games People Play (The Psychology of Human Relations).

Finally, a similar variation of the above theory, is 'I'm OK You're OK', which posits that people tend to hold one of four 'Life positions':

1. I'm not OK – You're OK.
2. I'm not OK – You're not OK.
3. I'm OK – You're not OK.
4. I'm OK – You're OK.

(Harris, 1973, p. 42)

In dispute resolution practice, the last of these positions is eminently preferable, and certainly what we would expect to find in the list of mediator attributes. People who tend toward holding this position, assume, that at least until another person demonstrates unequivocal evidence that they are not capable of 'reasonable' and 'rational' behaviour, they should be assumed to be socially, emotionally and psychologically 'OK'. The third position starts from unquestioned self-superiority and an assumption that most other people are in some way or other expected to be incapable, inferior, unsafe and untrustworthy. A mediator with such attitudinal inclinations might tend to be drawn to the 'directive' end of the mediator style in practice and tell people what to do by way of a settlement, rather than the facilitative end of the scale. This latter style, adopted by the majority of trained mediators assumes, as does this book, that their role is to empower or re-empower the disputants to take control, and design settlements appropriate to their particular life-work circumstances and preferences. The first and second life positions can be understood as reflecting the somewhat depressive, 'half-empty glass' personality. Hopefully, a would-be LM may be able to find some other fulfilling activity, but, it is to be hoped, not that of mediation. In summary, to be an effective peacemaker, an LM will need to hold a belief that most people can be both rational and reasonable. This is not always easy, since, at initial contact, they may well be behaving in both irrational and unreasonable ways.

Reflective reading

To what extent do the theories of TA and I'm OK You're OK make sense to the reader in terms of defining and explaining a framework of constructive interpersonal communication? As mentioned at the start of the chapter, trained mediators differ in the extent to which they either fully understand it, or decide to share it as a theory with people in dispute. Either way, for the LM, it is recommended that they regularly observe everyday conversations, so as to be able to recognise potential 'crossed' transactions and their effects. In addition, it is recommended that they practice framing questions in an 'adult – adult' mode, since that is most likely to generate a positive and constructive response.

4 What Are the Known Attributes of Effective Mediators?

> At this point, the reader might find it useful to take time out, before reading on, and to make a few notes about what attributes they feel they have that might make them a potentially suitable LM. If this feels difficult, it may help to imagine what attributes they would hope for if offered help by a mediator, for example, a good 'listener'.

A scan of mainstream mediation literature reveals relatively little reference to this topic. Marian Roberts draws the same conclusions, very little has been written about the qualities of the mediator. One reason for this is the weight that has long been attached to the personal rather than the processual aspects of the role. Personal qualities, often elusive and idiosyncratic, are not easily susceptible to analysis. In such studies [perspectives of the parties] (e.g., Landsberger, 1956; Raiffa, 1982; Stulberg, 1981), a list of preferred qualities was identified as follows:

- Originality of ideas,
- Sense of appropriate humour,
- Ability to act unobtrusively,
- The mediator as 'one of us',
- The mediator as a respected authority (that is, personal prestige),
- Ability to understand quickly the complexities of a dispute,
- Accumulated knowledge,
- Control over feelings,
- Attitudes towards and persistence and patient effort invested in the work of mediator,
- Faith in voluntarism (in contrast to dictation),
- Physical endurance,
- The hide of a rhinoceros,
- The wisdom of Solomon,
- The patience of Job,

DOI: 10.4324/9781003317005-4

- The capacity to appreciate the dynamics of the environment in which the dispute is occurring,
- Intelligence (both 'process' skills and 'content' knowledge – knowledge that equips the mediator to ask penetrating questions, to be aware of subtle nuances and when artificial constraints are being erected. Such knowledge should not be used, however, for the purposes of serving as an expert who advises the parties as to the 'right answers').

(Roberts 2014, p. 167)

Reflective reading

The reader might find it useful to make their initial notes, to be able to rate themselves on the above, on a scale from 0 (very poor at this) to 5 (very good at this). This will provide a snapshot of which attributes, if any, need to be improved and developed. Typically these tend to be of the 'need to do more of' or 'less of imperatives'. It can also be interesting to ask a close friend or two to also rate you, provided of course that it does not result in a dispute between you based on the outcome.

Whilst this list may initially read as quite daunting, it is worth noting yet again, that they are to some degree, common attributes for most people, regardless of whether or not they have trained as a mediator. Generally speaking, they are the stuff of what many people are like and try to do with the family, with neighbours and in the workplace, to help keep the peace in often stressful work-life activities. For example, in the workplace, people often look to particular colleagues to demonstrate such attributes, to enhance productivity, sales, service effectiveness and customer care. That in turn links well with the personal beliefs and assumptions referred to in the introduction regarding an LM. Roberts last point is also very helpful since it underscores the idea that such attributes are not taken as being linked to advising the parties as to their options, any right answers, nor indeed telling disputants what they should do to resolve the dispute.

5 What Skills and Strategies Do Trained Mediators Use and What Is the Difference between a Skill and a Strategy?

In reading the following, it is worth reflecting on the extent to which these skills and strategies flow appropriately from the above aptitudes. A typical everyday definition would describe a skill as 'the ability to do something well', 'expertise or dexterity'. Similarly, a strategy is typically described as 'a plan designed to achieve a particular long-term aim'. What soon becomes apparent is that we can, with practice, develop a particular skill, for example, summarising effectively. *As will be seen in the next chapter,* it is possible to apply that specific skill strategically. So, what starts as a 'skill' subsequently becomes a 'strategy'. For example, when using the skill of effective summarising, it can be applied as a strategy, namely to demonstrate 'effective listening with understanding, and summarising', and then be able to suggest moving on to the next stage of creative, 'future-focussed option development'. In other words, it can be seen that developing the expertise to use a particular skill, can, in turn, lead to an ability to apply the skill purposefully and intentionally, to achieve a particular outcome objective. In this sense, skills and strategies, once separately defined, often become interconnected in practice. It is hard to conceive of any skill being 'applied in action', that would not have a degree of either minor or major strategic intent or outcome effect. Mediators aim to listen skilfully so that they fully understand those who are speaking. Through this process, speakers would hopefully perceive an LM as both skilful and interested in them as people, which in turn, will also help towards developing mutual trust and respect. From many years of anecdotal experience of study and work in the social sciences, such skills are by no means confined to professionally trained practitioners.

Eye contact

It is worth pausing here to explore further the question of eye contact. Appropriate eye contact does not mean fixed or staring contact, which could well be intimidating and discomforting. Comfortable eye contact tends to be variable. For example, people often tend to look away whilst

DOI: 10.4324/9781003317005-5

speaking – as if to enable the brain to formulate what it is that they want to say without visual distraction, and, once said, return to relaxed eye contact again. When working as a helper with more than one person it is also helpful to make periodic eye contact with the person(s) other than the speaker. In this way, we can maintain a feeling of contact, by sending a non-verbal signal. This signal can usefully indicate that we know they are still present, and may perhaps be getting restless and perhaps wanting to respond to what is being said. There are also very important cultural and gender differences in making eye contact, particularly between Western and non-Western cultures. This is too complex to explore here in much detail, but it should be understood and demonstrated when working with people from other cultural groups. Their cultural preference is often apparent by paying careful attention to their behaviour, for example, by observing how they make eye contact, their spatial social distance, (proxemics) — in other words by observing and listening outside of our own cultural identity 'box'.

Returning to listening *as a skill*, most of us understand how to listen well to each other when what someone is saying is important and attracts our interest and attention. Typically this would apply when listening to a partner, a friend, our children and indeed, to typical life-work situations and occupations. Sadly, most of us will have experienced being listened to badly, when a listener is evidently not interested and is giving typical non-verbal signals, such as a loss of eye contact, looking around at others, and checking their watch frequently. Another issue here is the contemporary pace and pressures of life — work roles and responsibilities, including the speed of social networking and technological communications. More detail about these communications systems and their impact on disputes will be covered later in the text. All of the above serves as a helpful reminder of what needs to happen when the LM knows that they need to listen as well as they know-how, especially when there are warning signs that a potential dispute may be on the horizon.

Use of questions – Open versus closed questions

As will be explored here, there are different types of question forms or styles, each of which will be valid for serving a specific purpose. Mediation practitioners soon learn the importance of using the appropriate question strategically and purposefully. Without a doubt, the bulk of the practitioner's most creative and productive work is done through the use of open-ended questions. Such questions gather vital information about the issues and problems being experienced by the client. They also indicate concern for, and interest in, the speaker by the helper, starting with the history of the dispute, what has been tried so far and their outcome hopes and goals. In terms of mediation practice, they also have the added advantage of reducing the risk of inappropriate problem-solving suggestions or worse still, advising as to potential settlement options. In general, open-ended questions begin with:

- What?
- How?
- Who?
- Where?
- When?

Sometimes referred to as '4XWH' questions.

Why is also a valid interrogative question but tends to be accusative, such as – 'Why do you do that when you know it is harmful to yourself and others'. It can be made more positive by asking '*What* is going on for you when that is happening'. As with many ideas covered in the text, it is worth practising these problem-solving questions in general in everyday conversations rather than only in LM encounters.

These open questions can be compared with closed-ended and possible embedded advice questions as follows:

- Have you?
- Did you?
- Will you?
- Could you?
- Were you?
- Should you?

Yet another advantage of the open question is that it requires the respondent to think beyond just a 'yes' or 'no' reply. There are many examples of good media interviewers that are worth watching and listening to, for their effective use of open questions. Occasionally they fail to do this and it is amusing when the response to a closed question is a simple yes or no, compared to the details they had hoped for. With open questions, the speaker may also find themselves thinking and replying in a way that opens up new perspectives or thoughts that have not been considered by them in their stereotypical 'cracked record' answers up to that point. The reference to TA covered earlier also applies to using open questions when in the 'Adult' ego state, as it is less likely to be 'contaminated' by the other more negative states.

Summarising

Summarising has over time, emerged as a metaphorical Swiss Army Knife, and potentially of the most powerful tool in the toolbox of the practitioner. It can be said that all of the tools in the toolbox have their own very special uses and applications. However, from many years of practice, alongside listening and question skills, the summary emerges as the highest in overall importance. Given that the summary may be one of the strategically more powerful tools, why might it be that it is so often neglected by experienced and otherwise skilful mediators? One of the most powerful inhibitors is probably anxiety about getting it wrong. Professional practitioners like to look and sound as though they know what they are doing. Indeed it is known that clients are likely to benefit from, and be reassured by, such manifestations of confidence and competence. As a consequence, a practitioner may fear failing to summarise accurately and hence risk appearing to be less than highly effective at their craft. However, given the potential importance and indeed strategic power of the summary, practitioners need to understand that such inhibitors are outweighed by the potential benefits. The more we practise summarising regularly, the more we will develop the skill. As with so many other skills covered in this book, it can also be practised and developed in other work, domestic or social activities because, as the old analogy puts it, 'practice helps to make perfect'. Even if mistakes are made in the summary, the client can usually be relied upon to correct them, especially if asked if their situation has been summed up accurately or, if anything important was missed out? Just as the Swiss Army knife, with its many and varied little tools, is so skilfully designed for special individual tasks, the following section contains some of the particular strategic functions the summary can perform.

Reflective reading

How far do the above core 'toolbox' skills sound familiar and make sense in terms of potential application to the role of the LM? The reader might also find it helpful to undertake a 0–5 self-evaluation of their existing skills, in terms of with 5 being very competent and 0 being not at all competent so needing significant further attention and practice. As has been mentioned elsewhere in this book, such regular practice is worth undertaking in general everyday conversations rather than as a novice LM in action.

6 Looking in Detail at What These Dispute Resolution Skills in the Mediators' Toolbox Are, and What Effect They May Have When Used Strategically

Listening skills

Over and above what has already been said, it is useful here, to explore listening in more detail, in particular, what is known as 'active listening', sometimes referred to as 'free attention'. Without a doubt, when exploring effective interpersonal communication, active listening emerges as perhaps the highest essential key ingredient. Ask most people caught up in high conflict or dispute what they needed most and, apart from perhaps a wish to win the argument, they will almost inevitably say they want to be listened to. Paradoxically, attentive listening is even important for disputants and negotiators who are determined to win, since unless they fully understand the goals and strategies of the other side, they cannot exploit any weaknesses in their opponents' argument. In reality, the majority of our waking hours are spent in listening activity, probably more so than any other form of communication. Good listening is at the heart of all effective communication, across all everyday activities ranging from home, communities, family and successful work and business life. Given that it is so much a part of our daily lives, may perhaps account for how at times, we fail to do it as well as we know-how. It could be argued that, if we did it well every minute of the day, we would fail to fulfil our multitude of life and work activities and responsibilities. As a consequence, we inevitably 'filter out' much of the extraneous communication directed at us on an average day. Sadly, this 'getting through the day' common psychological defence mechanism, will at times inevitably inhibit our capacity to listen well. Listening is unlike hearing, which is technically a biological and passive process. Unless a person has a serious hearing impairment or we are wearing ear plugs, it is impossible not to hear, our senses are constantly bombarded with ambient noise, sometimes known as 'white noise'. In short, listening is an active psychological and emotional two-way communication process, in which the listener intends to listen more than they speak. It can be said that, since we have two ears, two eyes and one mouth, we should try to use them in that proportion.

DOI: 10.4324/9781003317005-6

It could be proposed that 'how goes effective listening is how goes the mediation'

Common active listening blockers and enhancers

Before looking in more detail at the *how* of effective listening it may help to consider what things happen to get in its way:

- If the speaker is talking to us about a problem they are having, we may listen to 'fast-track' and formulate a reply, give advice, or be tempted to try to solve a problem for the speaker.
- Thought wandering or distraction, perhaps when what is being said reminds us of a similar personal situation or experience we or others have had in the past.
- Formulating potential next response stages, such as clarifying facts and details, or asking what has been tried already etc.
- Not having enough time to listen well and not being open about that with the speaker and perhaps look for a better time to meet
- Feeling that we have heard it all from them before and being bored, but not sharing this with the speaker for fear of upsetting them.

Active listening enhancers

- Switch off any existing distracting brain activities, or as is often advised when installing a new PC programme 'shut down any other programmes currently operating'.
- Various writers have described appropriate and physical body postures, often with very similar characteristics. For example, directly facing the speaker; using an open posture rather than with closed arms and legs; periodically leaning towards the speaker so as to endorse specific points; maintaining good flexible eye contact; appearing and sounding relaxed. Anecdotally, a relaxed tone and unhurried conversation style are known to have a mirroring and calming effect on the other(s) involved.

Engaging in dispute resolution can reasonably be described as 'an intensive interpersonal activity'. Sitting with arms and legs firmly crossed or behind a desk, may well non-verbally contradict any effort to appear as being 'open' to, or genuinely 'in the moment with' the speaker. It can help if as a listener, we relax and adopt an internal mindset that says, all I have to do for the time being is to listen and understand this person. Helping them to move on to how they want things to be different in the future and what will need to be done to achieve that, really can wait until we have fully demonstrated listening and understanding.

Questioning skills used strategically

When used in mediation and constructive problem solving generally, open questions are not asked in a linear style but in recursive cycles depending on the answers received. For example:

- What has been happening to bring you here?
- When did the problem(s) you have mentioned first start?
- How were things between you before this happened?
- Who else is affected by all this and in what way?
- What have you and others tried to do about it so far?
- What happened when you tried that?
- Who else if anyone can you think of who might be able to help?
- How best do you think such a person or people could be asked to help?
- If that seems a good idea, when and how will you approach them about it?
- What, if anything might get in the way and stop that from happening and, what might you do to prevent that?

What can be seen from the above questions is that they progress from history taking, towards a potentially detailed plan of action, and end with an analysis of what might go wrong to spoil the plan. It is not at all uncommon for similar ideas and plans to have been made before, yet fail for lack of an end-stage focus on agreed actions. Professional mediators in the early days of development in the UK tended not to record that detail with and for the clients. It was then noted that the plans often failed, particularly if one party still had a vested interest in sabotaging the plans. From the time that a written copy became more common practice – often referred to as an 'outcome statement or record' — plans tended to be more likely to work. Such a written record is not a legal document, but all parties knowing that they all have a copy, certainly had a beneficial impact. Anecdotal evidence from business meetings also shows that otherwise exciting innovative ideas for change often fall by the wayside, for a lack of detail regarding who is going to do what, how and by when. The acronym SMART objectives are every bit as useful in dispute resolution goal planning. These tend to differ according to the source but are readily summed up as:

- **Specific**: They refer to something explicit and avoid generalised or vague notions.
- **Measurable**: Measurability aims to quantify concrete outcome goals to be achieved, so that we know not only that they are met but by what dates.
- **Attainable**: Goals need to be realistically achievable, not some 'pie in the sky' unrealistic or idealised dream.
- **Relevant:** There's nothing more frustrating than setting goals that won't give any specific practical future benefit because they were the wrong goals.
- **Time-bounded**: Identifying a realistic time limit within which goals are expected to be finalised.

Anecdotally, as an experienced manager, the excitement of new ideas for change and developmental plans within many organisations results in a lack of successful implementation from a failure to consider what might go wrong. From the euphoria of such 'lightbulb' moments it needs to move into a phase of serious reflective discussion of what may go wrong with the implementation stage and what can be built in to ensure any such glitches are anticipated in advance. To paraphrase a popular analogy, if it is possible for something to go wrong then we can be sure it will go wrong.

All of the above list of questions can be asked of any individuals involved in a one to one at the assessment stage, or in joint meetings. The replies from either person will usually differ between the two types of meetings.

A useful tip for developing open-ended problem-solving questions is to practice them in everyday conversations, away from the pressure of a conflict situation. Then reflect on how that went, in particular, in terms of how hard or easy it was mentally to switch a would-be closed question to an open one. Such mental switching involves an internal dialogue that starts with an inclination to ask a closed question that quickly converts it to an open one. That may sound like a long process and delay, yet with regular practice, it will become an unconsciously intuitive skill.

As practitioners, we should never forget the principle, that the 'expert' in the problem is the person living with it. They know better than anyone else what that feels like from within their world view reality and circumstances, in a way that others may never comprehend. It is generally regarded by experienced helping professionals to never say 'I know just how you feel'. The reality is that even having had very similar experiences and circumstances such as loss, we can never know how it is for the speaker. The fact that they are, for various reasons temporarily disempowered from solving their problems, should never be perceived as incompetence on their part. Open questioning creates opportunities for them to 'think outside of their box', which up till then may have been temporarily constraining their problem-solving capacity. Anecdotally, a couple of examples of things people said after such problem-solving encounters are, when you asked me those questions, it really made me think. Working with a couple, the female partner said, you somehow managed to ask the questions that nobody else had ever asked us, and they needed to be asked. Another possibility here is that, at times, helpers are inhibited from asking very personal questions out of concern that may be too challenging or upsetting. A typical 'worst-fear' outcome is that it might cause an explosion of emotion or a walk-out. Such issues may arise where disputants have been 'skirting around problems' for fear of their reaction if asked – as if fearful of a seriously 'upset apple cart', or the opening of a 'can of worms' effect. That was certainly the case in the above example of questions that nobody had asked. In reality, the worst fear reaction rarely occurs. More commonly, the question just does not get answered directly, probably indicating that the respondent(s) were not yet feeling ready to open up on that. Such a hypothesis by the practitioner should be understood that less potentially intrusive questions need to be avoided at that stage. As with all of the above skills and strategies, the art is all in the timing. As one family therapist guru used to say, the right intervention at the wrong time is the wrong intervention.

Positional bargaining versus needs-led negotiations

A common characteristic of people in disputes and conflict is an early tendency to adopt a 'bargaining position'. Typically such positions are constructed around their individual history of the dispute, when, how and by whom it was started, and how it has escalated to the present. This history is akin to a highly idiosyncratic 'history book'. Next, they also tend to identify in detail what will need to happen to resolve the dispute — typically the fine detail of the settlement conditions. What soon becomes apparent is that each party's historical account and their outcome requirements are inevitably in complete contrast to the other(s). As a child at school, the author was led to believe that history books 'told the truth', especially those bound in fine leather covers. It took some years to learn that in reality, they told the truth according to the opinions of the writer of the time. In particular, disputants' histories typically define the other party as the problem, the bad, untrustworthy, amoral, untruthful, intransigent party etc. By contrast, that writer is usually self-defined as the opposite of all of these derogatory labels. As regards the settlement conditions, it is also highly likely that all of their demanded concessions will require changes only on the part of the other disputant. Finally, in this list of norms is an expectation by each that any reasonable impartial listener, friend, or indeed a judge, will believe their account, and find in favour of their position. One key ingredient in the early stages of engagement is to point out that the practitioner will not be making any such judgements. However, it is quite usual for one or other to say 'and don't you think I am right on this', hence they will need to be reminded that is not what a mediator is there to do. Given the histories and settlement expectations, early attempts to mediate will be typically characterised by this 'positional bargaining' pattern, often together with threats against the other disputant(s) — for example, legal action. Sadly, the courts' route all too often results in a lose-lose outcome for both sides. One such notorious example involving a dispute over the fast-growing Leylandii Cypress tree resulted in a long and costly series of court hearings. The final judgement led to the complainant losing all financial assets including their house, as a result of their legal representatives' fees and court costs. When mediation works well, there are two key strategies essential in the early stages. Firstly the parties need to be helped to shift from a 'position-led' discourse to a 'needs-led' analysis. In other words, what is it that each side wants and needs, to be able to move on towards a possible dispute resolution and settlement? In most dispute contexts such needs are likely to include, to return to a quiet, more peaceful, less stressful everyday life; avoiding wasting time and financial resources; productivity; and, if possible, restoring former good family, professional or neighbourly relationships. As Muslim friends and colleagues so evocatively put it – 'To spend time bandage the wounds' – for the benefit of friends, family, communities and colleagues caught up in the 'crossfire'. Interestingly within such cultures and faith that emerges as every bit as crucial a process as the settlement.

Used strategically the summary facilitates:

Active listening, particularly in the early stages of identifying, clarifying, understanding and being able to fully understand the issues. Through 'micro' summaries of the details of the speakers' 'stories', the LM can effectively build 'bite sized' pieces of memory data. A very common concern of trainees and novice practitioners is that they will fail to remember important facts and data. Their concern is frequently framed as a question as to whether it is OK to take written notes. To require some trainees to stop doing this is almost akin to tying their hands behind their backs, and it creates a sense of cognitive dissonance. So why is it so important not to be taking written notes, particularly in the early stages of the session? The answer to this question lies in the clients' need to know that they have the full and undivided attention of the mediator – often referred to by therapists as 'free attention'. At that particular moment in time, active listening is, for clients, potentially more important than facts, details or anything else. Hence the importance of the regular 'bite-sized' or micro summaries, in embedding details in the memory bank of the mediator. As already referred to, summaries can later be used to confirm facts and then perhaps if agreed, used to make a summary record.

Demonstrating listening with understanding

The importance of effective engagement with each party involves not just a memory-building process, but also the added importance of demonstrating this crucial sense of engagement. The development of trust between the mediator and each party is powerfully influenced by the extent to which the clients experience the principles and values of the process through the helper's actions. In other words, it is not enough for the mediator to be listening and understanding, the speaker must know and feel this to be so, and the periodic summary conveys this cogently. Until each party to a dispute experience being fully listened to and understood by the LM, they are unlikely to be ready to move on to engage in dispute resolution negotiations. 'Fitness' to negotiate is metaphorically akin to athletes' who need to train to a high enough level to be able to compete. It is a 'common human need' of all people, to be listened to and understood, even more so in situations of interpersonal conflict and dispute. People locked in the high conflict and emotion of a dispute have frequently lost the capacity to either truly listen to, or understand each other – hence the early need to be heard by an impartial and non-judging third party. It is as if each person has a head full of 'white noise' that emanates from endless attempts to win verbal arguments, each against the other. A subtext of this condition is inevitably to distort what the other says, in an attempt to score power points against the adversary. Every mediator experiences that magic moment when, during the summary, the clients' eyes light up affirmatively. They start increasingly nodding and sending verbal and non-verbal signals to the effect of, yes, you understand what I am saying, and where I am coming from. When all parties are signalling this all-important experience of being heard and understood, is the point when the practitioner potentially has permission to propose a move on to the next stage of the mediation process.

- **Checking for accuracy:** Periodic careful summarising allows for a process of checking and re-checking that the detail of each person's contribution is being heard accurately. This in turn offers the opportunity to correct any misunderstanding or misperception on the part of each other or the mediator.
- **Controls the flow:** Frequently a client 'given the floor' and the opportunity to 'tell their story', will want to deliver a long and very detailed monologue. This has usually been long-rehearsed, developed, embroidered and adapted from the many conversations they have had with friends and supporters. The experienced practitioner knows that it can be difficult to staunch this flow, and the risk is that the other party will start to become alienated and feel 'negatively positioned'. The longer the first party holds the stage, the more the other is deprived of the equal opportunity to tell their story without adding defensive rebuttals, counter-claims and accusations made by the other. Novice mediators frequently identify this as a serious dilemma. How do they break into the monologue without risking offence or accusations of insensitivity? The use of frequent mini-summaries can be a particularly effective way of breaking up the monologue and engage the speaker in helping the mediator to understand fully what is being said. Typically what a mediator might then say would be something like, You are giving me lots of information here and it's important to me to be sure that I am following it accurately. So let me sum up what I think I have been hearing and learning so far. It can be seen that the values embedded in this intervention demonstrate respect for those speaking, together with a wish to be helpful by fully understanding them. In other words, it demonstrates that we care enough about them, and what they have to say, to slow things down. Such an intervention may well not work immediately, but in most instances, it will eventually have the desired effect. Having created a temporary breach in the monologue, the mediator can follow through with something like, OK, so I am sure that there is lot more that you would want to add but perhaps before you do that, I could just go to the other person, to give them the chance to say a bit about what has happened to bring them here. I will then come back to you so

that everybody has had a chance to say what they need to say before we move on.

- **Reflecting content and meaning:** People have the opportunity to hear their thoughts reflected by an impartial person, perhaps for the first time, in contrast to their repetitive 'internal script' or 'cracked record'. This reflective effect can also enable reformulations of previously rigid perceptions and, may bring a deeper understanding to the speaker. Often a client will say, well yes you are right about what I said, but listening to what you just summarised, makes me realise that it's not exactly what I really meant. That response recalls the charming story of the young child, who when asked by a teacher what they thought about a particular topic, responded with, I'm not sure just what I feel about that until I hear what I have to say about it.

- **Conveying beneficially neutral information to other parties:** In the act of summarising one party's story directly to them, the practitioner facilitates a more neutral and uninterrupted listening by the other party. While retaining the essential substantive and emotive content, the mediator is nevertheless able to 'launder' out some of the more toxic 'triggers' and 'barbs', which can so frequently inflame the reactions of the other party. As mentioned earlier, it is very common to find that parties in dispute have lost the capacity to listen actively and openly to each other. To paraphrase an old police caution — anything the other says may be taken down, distorted and used in evidence against them. It is as if messages to and from the disputants are passed through a negative defensive filter by the receiver, and translated to fit each person's historical position. Consequently, the process of summarising by a mediator has the effect of enabling each party to listen to the other, more attentively and potentially unconditionally, via the mediator. From extensive practice experience, it seems likely that this process of third party verbal transformation, has a significantly beneficial impact on the subsequent willingness of the parties to move to the negotiation stages of the mediation process. Important negotiation and mediation principles are also being imparted through this process – for example, turn-taking and even-handedness. Whatever the level of animosity between the disputants, each will likely have a vested interest in being seen by the helper as a reasonable, rational and ethical negotiator, so this is helpful to the process.

- **Marking the transition between stages:** The summary can be used to signal the appropriate points at which to move disputants through the stages of the mediation process. This transitional process is not always something that simply happens by chance. It often requires firstly an assessment of the parties' readiness to move on and, secondly, a verbal cue or proposal from the mediator. An example of such a signal by the mediator might follow an in-depth summary for each of the disputants followed by something like, so if you each agree with my summaries of what has been happening so far, maybe this would be a good point to move on to explore how each of you would like things to be different from now on. The response by the parties will confirm or not the validity of the mediator's judgement about timing.

- **Re-directing past-negative to future-positive**: In summarising the content of a complaint by each person about the behaviour of the other, the mediator goes on to check to confirm levels of understanding. For example, in a workplace dispute, one person may complain that scheduled departmental meetings never happen, because the manager responsible is too disorganised. As a result, staff grievances and problems never get aired or resolved. Rather than summarise it in that negative context, the LM could reframe it with something like, so as I understand it, you are thinking that, if these issues are to be resolved amicably between you in future, you would want to be confident that departmental meetings would happen on the times and dates as are agreed. In a neighbourhood dispute example, it might be, so it sounds like in the past there has been some upset about noise levels, parking, or play space. That leaves me thinking that it might be good if you could all think about exactly what you would want to be different in future, and who would have to do what if you were to be able to reach an agreement together. In a family context, It sounds like there have been some problems about the support payments, and how you both communicate about that with each other, and that in turn, this is having a worrying effect on the kids. So it sounds like it would be really good for all concerned if you could each think about what concrete actions could be put in place from now on, to begin to resolve these things between you? See more later on ideas on reframing.

- **Maintaining process management:** This helps all involved to remember where they are up to in the stages and checks any tendency for either person to detour, sidestep or move back into a focus on negative issues. As an example, correct me if I have missed something but I thought we had agreed that we had covered the first three points on the original list, and we had agreed to move on to the next item. What do you want to do, carry on with where we are now or go back to one of the earlier items?

- **Providing something to do or say when you are stuck for something to do or say:** Even the most experienced of mediators will occasionally have those dreadful and potentially de-skilling blank moments – the equivalent of the actor 'dying on stage'. Quite apart from breaking an uncomfortable impasse or 'stuckness' silence – as opposed to a constructive and contemplative silence – the use of a summary can often stimulate new ideas and questions. It can re-frame perceptions and 'lost' issues, alongside ideas for movement, for the mediator or either of the parties. There is no reason why this should not be initiated by the LM who might say, this all feels quite stuck just now, so why don't you each say what you think you have been able to clarify, and what if anything you have agreed so far. That may help you be clearer about where you might want to go from here. Note here that it may not be helpful to say 'I feel stuck' or 'you seem stuck' but to externalise the problem away from you or them as an '*it*'.

- **Closing or opening a session:** The 'where are we up to' summary can remind people about time limits, or the need to draw the session to a close and lead to the stage about what will be recorded as proposals and agreements. At the start of a further meeting, it can be repeated as a process of re-orientation and, yet again, lead to either confirmation or challenge by either party about the last meeting recorded outcomes.
- **Recording the outcome:** Practitioners often end a session with an overall summary of what were the main issues; what if any options were considered; what proposals had been agreed upon; who has agreed to do what, where, how and when; and any principles that emerged in the negotiations. Principles statements can be very beneficial, especially when arguments begin to become repetitive and circular. They are often encouraged in commercial and arbitration work in terms of benchmarks, by which any outcome settlement can be assessed. An example of such an agreed principle might be, that we agree to work towards a settlement that has the best interests of us all, will ideally minimise distress, or waste of resources and assets. In conclusion, it can be seen from the above, what a multi-faceted and strategic skill summarising is in the mediator's toolbox. The earlier reference to common reasons for summarising has developed into more than a dozen particular strategic uses – hence perhaps justifying its title as the 'Swiss Army Knife' of the skilled practitioner.

7 Some Additional Strategic Interventions beyond the Core Toolbox Skills

Normalising

Typically, when a dispute has reached its peak of apparent intractability, disputants tend to have reached a sense that their dispute is unsolvable, and hence is axiomatically *un-resolvable*. After all, if it were resolvable, as good problem solvers, disputants would between them have found a solution themselves. An example of normalising used by professionals, which might be used in many different mediation contexts, might go something like, well given what has been happening so far, I guess that it's not surprising that feelings and emotions have been running high between everyone involved. Such feelings often lead to frustration which in turn can lead to anger, upset and threats, back and forth, because that's what naturally happens in these sorts of situations. Sometimes, when these things get really bad, and everything that has been tried doesn't seem to have any effect, it can all feel hopeless and potentially insoluble. I guess what we are trying to do here is to look again at the problems and to help you all to get back in touch with your ability to resolve things together. Hard as it may be for you to imagine, most people do manage to get through it, and sort things out together. That doesn't mean it will be easy and there is no magic wand solution, but in this case, from what I am seeing and hearing so far, the odds, are potentially looking promising. Provided that this last comment sounds respectful and genuine, it can provide a much-needed touch of 'buoyancy', hope and optimism to reassure disputants.

Finally, it can be argued that unless people caught up in disputes and conflict gradually begin to experience doubts about the fixed positions they have adopted, they will not be psychologically or emotionally 'fit' enough – as referred to above under listening – to work on negotiating a settlement resolution.

Mutualising

As with normalising, it is quite common that by the time disputants reach a point of seeking help, positions have become deeply entrenched, and include a sense that they no longer have anything in common whatsoever.

DOI: 10.4324/9781003317005-7

The skilful and active listening practitioner is, however, likely to gradually pick up examples of mutual ideas, concerns, wants and needs. This might be summed up by practitioners as, from what has been said so far, it seems that you are each a long way apart in terms of what has happened to cause problems between you, and what needs to be done to make things better. When saying that it helps to reinforce the point non verbally by positioning hands wide apart. However, despite that, what I have noticed is that you are also very close together on certain other things, now the hands can be brought very close together. For example, such reflections might include:

- In general dispute contexts, whatever the outcome settlement, ideally, previous good relationships could be restored, and the outcome agreement be seen by all as fair.
- **Workplace**: That teamwork at all levels could be back to normal as soon as possible with no loss of staff, income, wages or productivity.
- **Neighbours**: That all involved can get back to more peaceful times, and restoring of previously good relationships. Where appropriate, neighbours can perhaps even consider working together to lobby other responsible people, and agencies, that may be responsible for such as soundproofing properties, parking, play-space, refuse collection and street lighting etc.

    Anecdotally, where this latter option happens it often has a powerful impact on the hitherto conflicted disputants. It transforms and relocates the causes and effects of the dispute to those rightfully accountable and responsible for dealing with such matters. It is also important that where neighbours band together to lobby those responsible; they carry more weight than any one as an individual. Community mediators have often been able to help facilitate sometimes multi-party neighbourhood meetings with a number of appropriate agency representatives.
- **Family**: That whatever happens, everyone is working together on what is best for the children; that they should be protected from emotional upset; overhearing arguments between you; still have very regular contact with you both, and maintain close links with extended family members and friends.

Reframing

Potentially, one of the hardest of all the skills and strategies that even very experienced practitioners often struggle to get right. Having said that, when timing and wording are right, it is also potentially one of the most powerful.

The objective of reframing is essentially to reformulate and transform a negative positional statement about why something cannot happen, will not be possible, or cannot be changed. The impact of these negatively framed statements can be of such power as to create an impasse, or stuckness, in negotiations and the search for settlement options. The reframe must be worded in such a way as to demonstrate respect for the person taking the negative position. A fairly straightforward response example might be something like, it sounds so serious right now that it could be a great relief for all concerned if a way through the problems could be worked on together. Maybe you could say more about what you fear might happen *if* you agree to any particular proposal that is causing you concern. Note that at this stage we are using the potentially less threatening *if* word. Once the person concerned has clarified the reasons why in their view the option would not work, we can move to say something like. So *when* you can consider a way forward, you would need to be very sure that the details include some certainty and reassurance, about the particular issues you have just described as worrying you. Strategically, this can be understood as a paradoxical 'yes' question, in so far as it is quite hard to answer with anything other than a yes. A yes may well be accompanied by a potential rebuttal such as, yes but I can't see how we can get those problems resolved, given how complicated it is for the other people involved to cope or manage the problems. A particularly strong case example in family mediation involved a young couple, with a baby girl just a few months old, but who had never lived together. The mother was still hurt and angry that the father had left her for a new girlfriend. Her key objection to the father having unsupervised was that he had never had the practical care of the child, so would not know how to look after her. The practitioner's initial reframe was along the lines of, I'm just wondering how important you think dad is to your daughter and her future, and for her to be able to see him regularly? As with the above comments about the 'yes' question, happily, in this case, the response was affirmative, albeit with a somewhat predictable further 'buts' about how he did not know how to do that. The follow-through reframe question was, so when you agree to arrange solo contact by dad, you would need to be very reassured that he knew how to provide a good safe standard of all aspects of practical care for his daughter. Note how the reframe moved on from *if* to *when*. The next level of reframing was, OK, so assuming that you, like any new parent, had to learn how to do that, who else could help him learn to do that? Note how the potential impasse had now moved to a 'future focussed' problem-solving mode. In reality, the mothers suggested and preferred option was that she could show him how at her home. Anecdotally, this can sometimes be a complex issue, where the mother may be hoping that in doing that, she might be able to persuade him to restore their relationship. In encouraging the exploration of other potential helpers, they may consider an NHS worker such as the health visitor. In some instances, the relationship between the father and maternal grandparents is positive enough for them to be an option, and similarly, possibly the paternal grandparents. Whatever any plan might involve, progress can then explore a time span of action and further key details. One other family dispute involved a child of around six years who need complex medication to be administered, whenever she had a potentially life-threatening episode. The same staged formula as above was used and with equally good results. Some practitioners question the potential risks of asking the above first question, regarding the importance of the other parent to the future of the child, and ask what if they say 'no'. In reality, if that 'no' comes from a deep-seated conviction, that the other parent is both unimportant and incapable of ever becoming a safe parent for contact then, in reality, mediation may well be a waste of time. Either way, to press on with negotiations regardless, unless both parents are jointly committed to making it work, there may be no guarantee that a child safeguarding and a risk-free contact plan ensured. Consequently, a safer alternative may be indicated, such as expert child care assessments and perhaps legal proceedings.

Concatenation

Typically described as a series of ideas, or things that are connected and also often refer to as chain-like linkages, which in turn suggest an analogy of the strengths of chain links being both flexible and yet strong in terms of effect.

From the author's many years of 'reflective practice', it began to occur that each of the above individual skills – when used strategically and with good timing – is likely to have a beneficial impact on the incremental process and stages of mediation. This in turn led to the hypothesis that when they were linked together, the effect became 'greater than the sum of its parts'. For example, after giving good accurate and acceptable in-depth summaries to each participant; a normalisation; followed by a mutualisation; and reframing, can then progress to a proposal. For example, assuming all involved were in accord with those comments, it could be a good point to move on to consider ideas for potential options and settlements. Again, as mentioned above, experience suggests that clients do not naturally move between the various stages of the process from first contact to agreement stages, so it may be appropriate for the practitioner to suggest the next step. If the suggestion is premature, one or other clients may say so, or possibly revert to circular arguments, which might be evidence that they are not yet feeling adequately heard and understood by each other or the practitioner.

Going with the resistance – The Jujitsu approach

Many years ago one of the author's sons was involved in a range of martial arts including Judo Jujitsu, Karate and Aikido. Whilst there are some common themes running through these, there are also different beliefs and objectives. For example, a key philosophical objective behind *Aikido* is to overpower opponents without doing them physical harm. During the many discussions about the work of a mediator and the son's hobby, in particular about managing resistance, some strong analogies between the two were identified. In short, rather than attempt to resist a positional disputant's argument by retaliating with a counter positional argument, often referred to as 'push – push-back', the art is to 'go with' the pushing energy. In the case of the Aikido philosophy, the one being pushed instead of using energy to push back, would step to one side, take the arm of the opponent and use the latter's pushing energy as a lever to cause them to fall. The function of the continued arm holding helps to avoid sustaining physical harm. Translating that into mediation the practitioner would respond to a 'push-argument' by saying something like, that sounds interesting. Do tell me more, and help me understand better what is behind your thinking and about your position. What is it that you are particularly concerned about and what you think might go wrong, if you followed the road currently being considered? Returning to the Aikido analogy, this would be the psychological equivalent of moving to the side of the opponent and walking beside them to take a new positional view of how they were viewing the landscape. Anecdotal experience on this idea came particularly from ten years of lecturing in a university, with adult students. The majority of the students had been in a range of social care work roles for several years without having any formal qualifications. The impact of the ideas and theories under debate was such that their daily hands-on work experience far outweighed that of the lecturer, and was often at variance with the theories being explored. In reality, it was fair to assume that the 'truth' lay somewhere in between their daily work experience and the theories at issue. In the process of metaphorically walking side by side, whilst talking and listening together, we would uncover perspectives, that more often than not, demonstrated contextual differences, rather than facts or truths. In other words, whilst theories can be useful generalisations, they may be at risk of becoming stereotypes, which can at worst, develop into poor practice and prejudices. We should never forget either that theories, particularly in social sciences, are usually transitory and not 'cast in stone'. In most instances of applying this martial arts strategy, it was usually possible to reach a level of agreement with the potential validity of both practice and theory perspectives and move to an acceptable combination of ideas. Circumstances and ideas usually alter cases and have significant application consequences. It is worth noting from the above experience that a class of 30 students would be closely monitoring such student-tutor exchanges, to assess the attitudes and level of respect for their experience. Any attempt to require uncritical adherence to a theory, whilst taking less time, may well have been futile.

How to undermine the rigidity of positions, whilst never undermining the people who bring them to the dispute. In other words, the problem *is* the problem, not the people so, work hard on the problem, and go easy on the people.

It is possible to propose that unless we find strategic ways of gradually and respectively creating doubt and uncertainty – sometimes referred to as psychological 'cognitive dissonance' – in the minds of the disputants – the latter will be unlikely to be ready to negotiate changes. Many of the strategies described above are designed to engender a gradual and progressive sense of uncertainty, for example, through the strategies of mutualisation or reframing. Anecdotally from practice, it is possible to observe non-verbal indications when this transformation is happening. A facial expression of confusion as one or more disputants review the pros and cons between their original 'positional certainty', against the 'new construct(s)' being presented to them. Once an optimal number of hitherto rigid positions are looking and sounding potentially less viable or sustainable, it may be possible to strategically invite a move to the next level of the resolution stages, that of 'creative option development'. In other words, using the aforementioned 'in-depth' summaries and concatenation, it can be suggested that this might now be a good moment to move on to consider some future-focussed options for change. It is usually worth emphasising that all such options and ideas should be listed 'without censure', before each one is subsequently analysed in a 'cost benefit' style, as to most or least liked and potentially viable. If this imperative is not proposed, it can be very frustrating, if every creative offering results in an instant negative reaction, particularly if one disputant is making significantly more suggestions than another. The subsequent systematic analysis will often change the options for the better, or trigger other new ideas for constructive change. All being well, a shift to the final stage, will hopefully involve drafting the outcome 'agreement' or plan, which should give clear details of what is to happen, and when, how and what actions will be taken by all involved. Since it can be assumed that the parties are at this stage are at their collaborative best, it is also worth including any concerns about what might go wrong and what can be built in to problem-solve any such 'worst-case scenario' snags – for example, traffic delays, mobile phone flat batteries, illness etc. This idea is often known as 'reality testing' and can lead to beneficial planning to enhance the prospects of a positive outcome.

8 The Power of Apology and Reconciliation in Mediation

Terms such as apology and reconciliation are not commonplace in the everyday language of professional dispute resolution and mediation. This is probably in part because, in its early days of mediation development in the UK, they were regarded as being too associated with therapy, rather than future-focussed negotiations for a settlement. Nevertheless, anecdotal evidence from practice over time suggests that both can have a significant positive benefit for people in conflict.

Saying sorry

Sorry is a very interesting word, because it is so commonly misused in everyday communications, and yet seems so hard to say at times when it is most needed. Its misuse can often be heard, for example, when someone bumps into us, perhaps whilst busy staring at their mobile phone. When that happens, it is often we who say sorry. However, at times when it is most needed in disputes and conflict, it can be what is so often called, 'the hardest word'. Why might this be? What follows is an exploration of some of the reasons because of which people may, or may not say sorry, alongside a closer look at what constitutes a genuine apology.

A common definition of an apology is, to acknowledge and express regret for a fault without defence. These last two words 'without defence' can be seen to feature negatively in the key elements of a genuine apology. One writer usefully defines the three key elements as:

a) **Acknowledgement**: A ritual whereby the wrongdoer can symbolically bring themselves low - in other words, the humbling ritual of apology, the language of which is often that of begging for forgiveness.
b) **Affect**: In order to truly accept responsibility the offender must also be visibly *affected* personally by what s/he has done.
c) **Vulnerability**: The offending party is placed in a potentially vulnerable state in offering the apology knowing that the chance exists that it may be refused. More than anything else, it is vulnerability that colours apology.

DOI: 10.4324/9781003317005-8

This author goes on to explore the potential application of these ideas to mediation and comments, apology, however, is clearly not about problem-solving. Nor is it about negotiation. It is, rather, a form of *ritual* exchange where words are spoken that may enable closure. There is often a felt need for some acknowledgement of the harm done; a need for some acceptance of personal responsibility for the injury inflicted, in short, an apology (Schneider, 2000, p. 1).

Here again, we see an expressed disclaimer against its application in problem-solving or negotiation. However, anecdotal evidence suggests that whilst such important principles often serve as good 'servants', they can also at times, if applied too rigidly, become 'bad masters'. Such a maxim does nevertheless signal a warning to 'proceed with caution'. The possible facilitation of apology in dispute resolution practice also needs to carry a caution against any evangelical conviction in its application. Apology and forgiveness are highly personal and idiosyncratic processes, emotionally and psychologically and should never be coercive or imposed by practitioners. Whilst space here prevents more detailed explanation, there are also significant cultural differences in its importance and these are explored in greater depth for practice application elsewhere (Whatling, 2021, Chapter 5).

So what factors might make it hard for a would-be apologiser to take the risk? Typical concerns might be:

- Will I be able to find the right words?
- Will my apology be rejected out of hand so that I lose face?
- Will it be used against me in the discussions and/or the final settlement?
- Will it be reciprocated, where I believe that the other side has also offended me?

For the 'injured party', the concerns might be:

- Am I prepared to consider fully accepting an apology?
- Would it help me and my situation?
- Is the time right, or are my emotions still too raw?
- How will I know it is really meant and not just a trick to get the other off the hook?
- Will it mean that what happened and all the hurt that I experienced did not matter?

From anecdotal experience, the person wanting an apology may not typically express their need for that directly. More commonly they will say something like the other person has never acknowledged just how much they hurt me, how hurtful it felt inside when they did or said that and how shaming it was for my self-esteem. As a consequence, it becomes important to 'listen outside of the box' and be ready to hear what can metaphorically be described as 'an apology waiting in the wings to be invited to come on stage'.

There are a couple of very key issues regarding the wording of the apology in terms of its acceptability to the receiver, and many people, get it wrong. The most common example, and to be avoided at all costs, is the little two-letter word *if*, when the four-letter word *that*, should be used. For example, 'I am sorry *if* I offended or hurt you'. This toxic two-letter word is often used in an apology when an offended person or group has already made it very clear that they have truly been offended and hurt. History over time lists many famous people, who made their situation infinitely worse by the 'if' word. This list has included high ranking members of faith groups, popular media personalities and politicians worldwide. Many such examples made their situation worse by refusing to apologise at all, despite widespread public evidence of their hurtful actions and words. Why might it be that such influential figures were reluctant to say sorry? The most obvious answer is that they feared it might tarnish their reputation, that they may lose face. Again, as mentioned above, there are very significant differences within different cultures. Anecdotally, those that did genuinely apologise often found that they attracted greater respect for their honesty and humility. Another common reason for reluctance is the fear of adverse legal consequences if the matter goes to litigation. Space here is too short to look at this issue in much depth, but professional bodies such as the General Medical Council in the UK have over recent years, increasingly encouraged their members to say sorry. The actual wording of apologies in such professions, especially when in writing, may be a matter of concern. However, to say something like 'We are really sorry that we were unable to save your loved one', is very different from an admission of medical negligence. Many years ago, the author working as a consultant to a major urban UK health service patient complaints consortium, reviewed their research study of complaints.

Practitioners' primary 'worst fears' concerns related to the risk of formal time-consuming complaints procedures and costly legal compensation claims. To their surprise, the substantial majority were related to the practitioners' communication rather than clinical practice or diagnosis. Many in the study wanted an apology, including a hope for the restoration of a previously good patient-doctor relationship, and there was often the hope of improving the standard of practice for other patients in the future. Any reference to financial compensation came at number seven on the list. Finally, on this issue, there are numerous examples of countries, including the US and UK, increasingly passing legislation that prohibits any information given in an apology, including in writing, from being subsequently admissible as evidence in litigation. It seems clear that facilitating an apology for an impartial and trained mediator, whilst complex, is likely to be significantly more difficult for the LM where directly involved in the dispute. The wording of any request for an apology, or offer to give one, will rest heavily on a careful choice of words, see above for the importance of a needs-led dialogue as opposed to threats or 'positional bargaining'. Equally, any attempt to trade an apology for any other concession is unlikely to go well. Conversely, anecdotal experience shows that, if framed in accordance with the principles described above by Schneider, the constructive and positive impact and reaction on the receiver(s) will often demonstrate surprisingly substantial benefits, hence it has often been referred to as 'the power of apology'.

Reconciliation

As with apology, reconciliation is rarely identified as an outcome objective or explored in professional mediation practice. Despite that, anecdotal experience shows that it may well bring a serendipitous bonus, especially when, though not inevitably, when associated with an apology. It is not surprising that conflict in everyday life creates significant upset, both for those directly involved and those around them in the family, community and workplace. Family friends and associates frequently become drawn in and typically tend to take sides. The impact on social relationships and networks quickly spreads, often with very negative effects on all, like the ripples from a stone in the water. By way of an example often used in training, one neighbour, Pete, owned a sailboat normally kept in his drive. The other neighbour, Tom, had an unused garage, so he offered its use to Pete for the boat, to protect it from bad weather and the risk of theft. Tom and Pete had enjoyed a good longstanding neighbour relationship. They played sports together, their wives were very close and enjoyed regular social time together, and the children played together regularly. Both families had also enjoyed regular use of the boat, together and separately. Sadly, one night a fire started in the garage causing significant damage to both the garage and boat. The value of the boat was estimated to be around £8000–10,000. Repair costs were estimated at £5000–6000, which was also the estimate for repairs to the garage, the insurance of which unfortunately did not include contents. Neither was the boat insured for fire damage. No cause for the fire was identified by the fire service, a general assumption being that it may have been a wiring fault. In the days that followed, Pete made it known that he expected Tom to pay the repair costs on the boat, on the basis that he had failed to insure the garage for contents. A subscript for Pete was that unbeknown to anyone, he had accrued some significant debts in launching his business, and had been contemplating selling the boat to cover the debts. He certainly had no spare cash to pay for the repairs. Tom, however, held the view that he had been doing Pete a favour by letting him use the garage at no cost, and Pete should have comprehensively insured the boat to include fire damage risk. This dispute quickly escalated into a conflict, with Pete and Tom no longer able to discuss the issues without verbal arguments and threats about potential legal claims action. Typically this tends to be known by mediators as the parties being stuck 'in their positions'. The impact on the family and friends was typically very upsetting, with wives feeling duty-bound to support their partners, and hence no longer able to enjoy their hitherto happy social relationship. Sadly too the children felt caught in the middle and had to take the side of, their waring parents, to the extent of no longer playing together, nor even sharing seats on the school bus. This training exercise was used in two parts. Part one involved a role-play in which Pete and Tom were seen by an arbitrator, who in about ten minutes would hear their individual accounts of the issues. At the end of this stage, the arbitrator would announce their decision as to the financial settlement, which would be final and legally binding. During this stage, neither party was allowed to speak to the other, only to the arbitrator. The latter could ask questions of each to clarify any details. Anecdotally, it is quite common for disputants to assume that arbitrators and judges have some sort of rule book, or 'yardstick', by which to declare some standardised judgement. In reality, other than some general principles such as 'duty of care', this is not so. It is more commonly an issue of personal professional values and opinions. In the above case, even 'duty of care' opinions may differ greatly in litigation, in terms of which individual had exercised the least greater or lesser care. As a consequence, when the role play settlements are announced, they can vary from one extreme to the other, including one party having to pay the full amount, a 50/50 split, neither having to pay anything and a variety of amounts either way. In the dispute litigation field, it is well known that each party to the dispute, if considering legal action, tends to believe that their case is by far the stronger and hence, worth the risks. In reality, they are effectively gambling by believing that the odds will be in their favour. Round two of the exercise leaves the disputants in each group as before but the arbitrator now taking the role of mediator. This time, anyone can speak to anyone and the mediator is instructed neither to suggest options, give an opinion as to right or wrong, nor to determine a settlement. Instead, they must do everything possible to encourage the parties to talk together in an attempt to find an acceptable outcome for all involved. Typically, each party tends to start by reverting to positional bargaining and attempting to persuade the mediator to see the 'rightness' of their case. Given that the mediator at this stage is still in training, this is not easy, but if struggling too hard, they can be slipped a note by the trainer, to suggest asking what each disputant needs as well as the family members, to find a fair settlement, and what future-focussed options they can explore as an alternative to litigation. Even within ten minutes, it is remarkable what variety of options can emerge. For example, both men could work together to repair the boat and so substantially save on labour costs. If they lacked the skills it may be that a friend or other family member could help. Tom could put up the finance for the work so that it could then be sold and the loan repaid from the profits. Tom could fund the repairs in return for a joint ownership arrangement from then on. The questions regarding family needs inevitably open up discussions about the negative effects on wives, children, other neighbours and friends, especially in close-knit cultures and communities. This in turn inevitably links to how many years those relationships had endured and the positive emotional network benefits for all concerned. Here too we can also see how the reconciliation bonus also comes to pass – often without any formal discussion. The settlement outcomes of both sessions are then written up on a flip chart, even if neither was finalised. The benefits of mediation over arbitration or litigation become immediately clear. Another interesting concept here is that the mediated settlement is regarded as 'fair'. See the earlier discussion regarding this notion of who can determine fairness. One final point in this exercise is that in round one, whilst an arbitrator or judge will probably impose a binding financial settlement, neither could in law have imposed any of the subsequent creative options identified by the parties. You cannot force disputants to work together on a boat or loan each other money.

9 Some Contemporary Issues and Dealing with Social Media Communication Conflicts

As mentioned at the start of this chapter, over recent years, particularly in workplace and family contexts, there has been a dramatic increase in disputes arising from modern technology communication systems such as texting and emails. This technology has resulted in a more abrupt and abbreviated language style, that lacks the quality of more traditional communications. Its often rushed and cryptic style may well unintentionally lead the recipient to feel offended and respond in retaliatory language and the beginning of a conflict spiral, especially when copied into communication with other work colleagues, family members or friends.

This new reality may well confront the efforts of the LM either directly involved, or close to others in dispute, so it may be worth briefly exploring this in more detail, along with some recommendations on how best to deal with it. Do you need to respond? Much hostile communication does not need a response. Letters from ex-spouses, angry neighbours, irritating co-workers, or adversarial legal advisers do not usually have any legal significance. Often, it is emotional venting aimed at relieving the writer's anxiety or frustration. If you respond with similar emotions and hostility, you will probably just escalate conflict without satisfaction, and get a new piece of hostile mail back. In most cases, you are better off not responding as suggested by one writer:

If you need to respond, I recommend a BIFF Response. Be Brief, Informative, Friendly and Firm (Eddy, 2007). Be brief – going into too much detail can at times result in a spiral of conflicted two-way communication. In the words of the old saying, 'least said soonest mended'. The same principle applies to the respondent. Not rising to the bait will often delete it from future reference. Be informative and friendly. Keep responses friendly, brief, to the point and factually informative. Avoid threats, or derogatory comments about the other person's behaviour, reputation or character. The longer you maintain the above principles and a respectfully assertive rather than aggressive manner, the harder it will be for the other person to respond negatively. Finally, be firm. In a non-threatening way, clearly outline and summarise. There are interesting links in this advice with what was said

DOI: 10.4324/9781003317005-9

above about Transactional Analysis, in that the longer you stay in 'Adult' mode the harder it can be for a disputant to respond negatively.

How to start and what to say

Much of the above text has included what to do when a disputant does certain things that are unhelpful and negative. Anecdotally, experience suggests that what most novice mediators want to know is, not only what to do, but also what to say at difficult times in the process. Hence, in concluding this chapter it may be useful to consider some helpful and constructive ways by which to approach a disputant as the LM in particular contexts.

- **Workplace LM:** It seems clear that things have not been going well between us, (or some members of the team), for some time and that is beginning to have a negative effect on team relationships. It feels to me that unless we try to sort things out that may well get worse and potentially damage morale and productivity. So I'm wondering if you might be willing to sit down and discuss how this has happened, and what we might decide can be done to get things back to where they were. If we were to be able to do that, we would need to listen carefully to each other and say what we each want from the other to be able to move forward together. How does that sound from your position?
- **Neighbourhood LM:** We seem to have been having some problems lately, in particular about (parking, noise, soundproofing, children's play space), so I am wondering if we could all get together and talk that through in terms of what we can do to manage things better as neighbours and families. I'm guessing that it is upsetting for all of us and that it would be good if we could get back to how things were before things changed. It may be that some of the particular things that are causing difficulties are beyond our ability to do much about in which case we could explore together what other responsible organisations could do to help with such as housing, play space, parking, soundproofing etc.
- **Family FM:** We both know that things have not been going well lately and that it's causing a lot of stress, and upset, not just for us but for all our family and friends. We have been under lots of stress lately here and at work and I'm guessing that we both worry about where this might all end up. I know for sure that I have not been helping, in the way I have behaved lately with the things I say and do, and I don't feel good about that. So I am wondering how you feel about finding time to sit down, talk together about these things and explore what could be done to get things back to where they were. I know it won't be easy for either of us. If we were to be able to do that, we would both need to listen carefully

to each other and feel and be able to say what we each want, to be able to move forward together and get back to how things were when it was good. How does that sound?

Reflective reading

The reader might find it helpful to think about how the other person might respond, and in particular if that is a negative reply, how to respond to that in a way that reflects what has been said in the text above, for example, TA.

As a general principle, it is important to monitor your reaction to a negative reply before saying anything that might escalate the dispute into conflict. If the immediate emotional reaction is to want to retaliate, the traditional advice about 'counting to ten' may be a good place to start. Even if attempts to respond well still fail, at least there will hopefully be a sense of having genuinely tried to do the right thing. Remember the importance of 'face', that is, the importance of understanding how the other person(s) may need to take time to save face before deciding how to respond. Anecdotally, in major commercial disputes, in the US, it is common for one side to consider what to do about the other side's 'face' need. In other words, what can they build into any settlement offer that enables the other side to look good, reasonable and responsible? In non-Western cultures, for example in Japan and China, face-saving is an extremely serious issue and can make or break any attempt at dispute resolution, especially in the commercial arena. A useful general principle is to paraphrase 'don't get mad, don't get even' – to 'get strategic'. In other words, stay calm and consider the best range of constructive responses. If we took just one of the above LM invitations to 'party', it may be useful to consider and prepare for how best to respond. For example in the case of a workplace dispute the reaction might be something like, who the hell do you think you are to be talking about sorting things out when you are one of the main causes of the problems between us in the first place? Apart from anything, you're not a manager in this department who might have to approve of, or implement any possible deal we come up with together, so what's the point in us talking? The reader might like to think at this point about how they might respond to such a reaction. As an example that seeks to draw in all of the ideas covered so far in the text, we might try, OK, firstly I'm sorry that what I said has left you feeling that I may be more responsible than anyone for what has been happening, and also I appreciate your point about my lack of formal power to implement any ideas about a potential settlement. What I would say is that if you will consider again my original suggestion I will be very ready to talk about and listen carefully to examples of my behaviour, that you and others believe has been contributing to problems, and I will aim to be very open to changing that behaviour. I would also say that in these situations, higher levels of management are often only too ready to accept proposals for change that were financially viable, especially if it improves team morale and productivity. Lastly, I would add that I am thinking you might need time to think over what I have said and if necessary, chat with others before deciding whether to talk more or not. How is that sounding now? If we deconstruct that response we can see that it starts with what is often referred to as taking a 'one-down'. In other words, to recap on the words of Schneider in the above section on an apology, a ritual whereby the wrongdoer can symbolically bring themselves low – and: ....offering the apology knowing that the chance exists that it may be refused. More than anything else, it is vulnerability that colours apology. Hard as it may be to adopt such responses in this situation, taking a one-down position is known to be a very powerful strategy. In terms of tone of voice, it must be truly meant, and in this case not least as it is probably to some degree 'true'. Next in the analysis of the proposed response is that it demonstrates to the objector, that they have been carefully listened to and their key points noted accurately. Their points can then subsequently be offered as possible goals for action, both for the respondent and potentially for higher management support. Finally, the offer of time to think brings the possibility of respecting face, rather than pressuring for a quick decision. Anecdotally, a common response to that suggestion will be that the other side will return at some point accepting the offer of talks They may well maintain that they believe their original position was the right one, but they will agree on the basis that it is in the best interest of all others involved in trying to sort things out. Finally, on the issue of management support for any 'deal', it may well be happy to endorse it since it may avoid any escalation in disputes, the potential involvement of the unions or loss of productivity.

Reflective reading

To what extent does all of the above ring bels with the daily work life experience of contemporary cryptic social media communications and how far does the text offer potentially useful advice on constructive responses? Hopefully too, the cross references to TA and apology are noted as well as the importance of face saving.

10 Some Cautionary Concerns Such as Ensuring Safe Practice

Different strokes for different folks – a twentieth century proverb meaning that different things appeal to different people. A brief overview of how mediators do what they do as practitioners follows, including descriptions of various procedural flexibility options. This chapter provides some potentially additional useful ideas and concepts that may not have knitted so well into the main texts but could be woven in by the reader.

Solo versus co-working

In the early stages of training, supervision and novice level there is often a significant benefit and reassurance from co-working with an experienced partner. There can be complications in terms of who takes a lead and turn-taking, so these matters need a significant amount of pre-session planning. In professional practice, there is also a cost resource issue for clients. As time moves on and confidence increases, it is common for practitioners to move to solo practice and so reduce costs and avoid the above partnership protocol issues. Another option, depending on particular case circumstances is 'shuttle mediation' whereby disputants are seen separately with the practitioner(s) moving back and forth between them. Again there are obvious time resource issues here and anecdotal evidence shows that the chances of an agreement are significantly lower than in face-to-face mediation. In part, this would appear to be linked to the likelihood that a settlement can be reached is significantly reduced where disputants are reluctant to talk eye-to-eye in the same room together. It also has an attendant risk of the practitioner assuming power as a go-between dealer or settlement broker. Nevertheless there are times when despite the limitations, it can be worth trying, particularly where conflict motions are high and there are potential risks of intimidation or violence. Interestingly, the UK Advisory Conciliation & Arbitration Service (ACAS), tended to use the shuttle as its common preferred option, with all sides only coming to a joint session when the settlement was already effectively agreed. More recent anecdotal evidence suggests a move more towards face-to-face meetings. Their website shows substantial advice and skills training opportunities centred mainly

DOI: 10.4324/9781003317005-10

on the workplace context. The costs, benefits – and the 'how to organise and manage' – practice working options and others not included here are described in much greater detail in Whatling (2021).

BATNA and WATNA – useful options to understand and consider when caught up in a dispute.

BATNA stands for the best alternative to a negotiated agreement and WATNA means the worst alternative to a negotiated agreement. The concepts described by Haynes and Haynes (1989, p. 11) are useful when engaged in a dispute and considering potential best or worst outcome possibilities. In other words – standing back from the heat of the fray consider what is the best or worst that could happen if things are not going well and may not work? There may well come a point at which a challenging cost-benefit analysis might be wise. One result of such analysis may be that disputants may decide to stop the conflict and just carry on living with the dispute circumstances – a BATNA decision. For example, many couples decide against the costs of separation and for the sake of the children to stay together, at least until the children are leaving home. Neighbours may decide to give up trying to win the fight over parking or noise and either live with it or move. Workplace disputants may decide to avoid contact with each other as much as possible, especially in the interests of productivity or look for work elsewhere. One unexpected consequence may even be that such a 'backing off' tactic results in the other side responding with a similar 'cease-fire' offer. To sum up, a BATNA, whilst not achieving the desired goal, may have none of the possible negative consequences – for example legal costs – of maintaining the fight at any cost.

Win-Lose. Lose-Lose. Win-Win.

These three potential dispute outcomes are common terms from the literature and practice in mediation. Win-Lose indicates that by going to arbitration or litigation one party will win and the other lose. Unsurprisingly, the loser is likely to feel aggrieved, not just about losing the argument but very possibly a significant loss of assets. They may well decide to challenge the outcome by an appeal, though all too often this can involve a lengthy delay with the attendant risk of further losses. Lose-Lose, as suggested, results in both sides losing not only their desired outcome but again, financially. Win-Win is frequently misunderstood, in that it is often taken as meaning both sides get what they wanted. In reality, it has come to be regarded professionally as a result, the total benefit of which is 'greater than the sum of its parts'. This relatively commonplace term is generally attributed to Aristotle and metaphysics. In this context, it describes a situation resulting from the positive consequences of disputants working together to identify potential positive beneficial outcomes that result in hitherto unforeseen bonuses. An example could be that in a major workplace dispute, the workers may threaten to walk off the job and stop production. In keeping with the positional, often threatening negotiations referred to above. The employers may retaliate by threatening to shut down the company and cease trading. The consequence of either threat becoming a reality can result in employees becoming unemployed, often with dire consequences for families – especially at times of and in areas of high unemployment. Equally, the company risks losing production, possible bankruptcy and consequential loss of substantial assets. By comparison, a period of constructive negotiations, typically between union and staff side members, can result in a win-win which, as referred to above, may include additional elements not previously considered to be 'on the table'. Anecdotally, apart from saving jobs and production, such deals can have included other unforeseen agreements, for example, in return for additional paid leave days or break times, the employers introduce an employee bonus scheme or company shares scheme, in return for increased production. Another variation that has appealed to workers can include a joint consultation process, commonly known as 'quality circles', resulting in a substantial production speed and quality rate. Workers who spend every hour of the working day making one single component, apart from being bored, are often found to have better ideas than Research and Development teams on how to improve not just speed but improved quality and durability of particular components.

'But me no buts' – How to avoid the negative impact of 'but', when 'and' works better

This phrase eloquently draws attention to the potential problems related to the overuse of the word 'but' in disputes and mediation. When we hear a manager saying, I may not have always been the best boss; or the neighbour who says, OK my kids are not little angels or the divorcee, I may not have been the perfect spouse, we know with a high degree of certainty that the very next word will be a 'but'. It is less than surprising that people in dispute will use this simple conjunction and yet it is also surprising how often it is used by mediators with clients. For example, I can see that you all have very strong feelings about what has been happening *but* perhaps we need to think now about changing how *we* could do things differently in future. Here too is another minor but quite annoying, the *'royal we'*, instead of *'you'*. By definition for people seeking help, it is they who need to start thinking about what needs to change from then on. Whilst 'but' is an innocent enough everyday conjunction, at times of high conflict and low trust, it has almost the verbal impact of the head-butt of the ram or the street fighter – a colloquial expression said to be the equivalent of the 'Liverpool handshake'. With a little practice, it is possible to largely eliminate *but* from our vocabulary because *and* is inevitably a less provocative conjunction. It also has the added benefit of implying a forward problem-solving momentum and potential optimism. Hence, we can simply alter the earlier example, I can see that you all have very strong feelings about what has been happening *and* therefore perhaps this might be a helpful time for you to think about how things might be done differently in future.

Empathy

The reader might find it helpful to consider how they might feel if someone close or directly involved with them in a dispute, approaches them and offers to mediate? That is what is known as a 'circular question'. In other words, it requires the reader or listener to put themselves in the position of another – and therefore get closer to understanding how they may be feeling – and in turn, how best to approach them. This questioning form is commonly used in dispute resolution. The impact is to help positional bargaining disputants think outside of their recursive 'stuck record' script, by having to think about how they might feel if they were in the other person's shoes. It is as if they then have to view the situation from a different place in the landscape, a perspective shift that may bring new and constructive insights into their own and others' wants and needs. Reflecting for a moment on the question at the start of this paragraph, when considering the possibility of intervening as a helper in a dispute, it might be wise to avoid referring to oneself as a mediator. Depending on the other(s) involved, that may sound as if the LM is assuming a higher level of competence or some sort of moral high ground. It might be wiser to simply enter the fray as an equal player and, what is often now referred to as 'walk the talk'. Start by inviting discussion around the things that have been causing difficulties recently, and to see what if anything can be tried to ease the tensions for all involved.

Practice makes perfect

This well-known analogy may help novices to take it easy on themselves on the road to perfection. A key concept here is what is referred to as 'reflective practice'. After every intervention, we could usefully take some time-out for a period of reflection. For example, what was done, said, tried, that seemed to be effective or not. If the latter, how that might be done differently, either more of or less of next time? People caught up in often bitter disputes can be difficult to work with, especially in the early stages of the process. Nevertheless, it can be frustrating to hear practitioners blaming the clients, and describing them as 'the clients from hell'. Equally, thinking: I am hopeless at this and probably always will be, is equally unhelpful, hence the need to try positive critical constructive reflection. From anecdotal experience, it is more often a case of mediators not yet having enough tools in their toolbox, to have had a positive effect this time. Fortunately, in the UK, trained competent and accredited mediators are required to have regular annual hours of supervision, including some directly observed client practice sessions. In addition, they must undertake regular 'continuing professional development' training. The reader, as a neophyte mediator, is unlikely to have access to anything like this level of professional help. Nevertheless, with luck, they may have trusted friends, partners and colleagues that they can call on for support.

Learning from the client

Always be ready for, and open to, learning from your client(s) and significant others. Some of the best learning experiences can come from how clients and colleagues react and what they say. One particular best example was when a trainee mediating particularly noisy high-conflict role-play disputants waited for some time before asking, is this what usually happens when you two try to talk about things? The disputants both cast their eyes to the sky and answered in the affirmative, each simultaneously accusing the other as always starting the rows. The student then asked, And does that help with the discussions? Again both confirmed that it never does. He then asked, so would you like me to stop you if I hear it happening again? To extend that excellent line of questioning, it could be extended a little further by adding, since it is obvious that you can do that at home, and it does not help. Since you have come to try mediation, maybe you could agree to do it differently here? This may not work instantly but after a few reminders, that they consented to, it is usually effective.

Humour

Used very carefully, respectfully and sensitively, humour can help in some situations. However, it all depends on how well the helper has come to know the disputants and, as the best comedians are always reminding us, it is very much about timing. If in any significant doubt about how it will be received, it is probably best avoided. For example, anecdotally a co-working mediator pair was observed using it repeatedly in the meeting. It not only sounded dreadfully patronising but, observing the reactions of the parties, caught up in the trauma and hurt of a divorce, it arguably amounted to professional malpractice. Happily, both elderly practitioners retired from practice soon after. If used at all, it is likely to be the exception rather than common practice. One successful case example was with parents in a lengthy dispute about contact over the arrangements for their three-year-old daughter, who lived with her mother. The father, frustrated by the mother's willingness to agree to any arrangement had taken the matter to court more than once and been granted contact orders. In mediation, the mother presented as very smart in a business style suit and sat mostly with her arms tightly folded, looking and sounding very unmoveable. She maintained her opinion that regardless of the court order, she refused to force the child to leave the house with her dad whenever he arrived at the front door as arranged. The father appeared to be caring and sensitive and fully agreed that no attempt should be made to force the child, regardless of the court orders. After lengthy discussions and attempts to explore potential options, for example, starting by meeting all together in a public place, it became clear that we were at a stalemate, often referred to as an impasse. In this real-life situation, both parents were then complimented about, what had been said so far, their daughter sounded very bright for her age. Clearly from her expression, the mother liked this and, smiling for the first time, she relaxed very slightly and spoke of how friends and family had noted this too, including at her playschool. The practitioner continued by commenting about how, for her young age, she also sounded to be quite strong-willed. Again mother responded by commenting that indeed, once their daughter made up her mind not to do something, there was little hope of budging her from that decision. The helper then asked which of her parents she most took after. The mother burst out laughing and pointed at herself and added, me of course. The atmosphere shifted noticeably from that moment. She unfolded her arms and relaxed in her seat in a far more open communicative style. Over the next few minutes, it was suggested that the parents were, by definition of the time spent caring for their daughter from birth, both were experts in what she needed and, even, at times, knew how best to persuade her to do things she perhaps did not want to do. The mediator added that Judges and courts had changed substantially over the years and were reluctant to make orders over residence and contact. If necessary they would do that and would demonstrate their care for children. Despite that, they could not be expected to love nor fully understand other people's children in the way that parents did. Consequently, for example, if a growing child declared that they no longer intended to go to school, accept medical treatment, or wished to play ball on the motorway, that would not be permitted by their parents. Given that they exhibited no disagreement with this train of thinking, it was then suggested that they may already have discovered times when they had to find clever ways of encouraging their daughter to do things she did not want to do. If not so far, given how bright and strong-willed she was, it would certainly be likely to come up as a problem in the future. Given all of that discussion, they were asked what they could think of, that might encourage the little girl to spend more time with her dad. Something that practitioners had also learned over time, is that it can very be hard for children and adults in such circumstances to climb out of the metaphorical hole they had dug themselves into, without losing face. The parents responded surprisingly well, with each reminding the other of examples of things that had worked before. This even included persuading her to go to a party which she had not wanted to go to, with the result that she had a great time. They did eventually come up with some initial tentative ideas with much of the lead being taken by the mother. A follow-up review reported that contact had been satisfactorily resumed. To sum up, what was happening here in terms of practice strategies? Firstly, the practitioner had avoided going head-to-head with the mother, but took more of a martial arts approach – referred to earlier – by getting metaphorically alongside her. Comments were made about how they mutualised their joint responsibilities; highlighting their wisdom as experts in their children; and the difficulties parents often face, which normalised their struggle. All of that careful 'groundwork' prepared the way for some creative option development, in a way that no court, nor pressure from the helper would have impacted. All of that strategy was also firmly rooted in an atmosphere of respect and earned mutual respect.

Timing

As with humour, most of what effective practitioners do is also about timing. It can be said that a potentially good intervention at the wrong time usually shows it was the wrong intervention. Most novice mediators worry about getting the intervention wrong and causing one or other disputants to get angry, feel offended, judged, or sided against. Assuming that nothing in the practitioners actions justified such a reaction, in the great majority of instances such negative responses do not happen. More often, what usually happens is that where the strategic intervention does not work and fails to get the hoped-for movement, the practitioner will know that the timing was wrong and probably premature.

So what? Some final key issues for the reader to consider at this stage

The question so-what in this instance is not asked in a stereotypical cultural sense as meaning, tough luck; deal with it; man-up; that's your problem; am I bothered? In this context, it is meant as a valuable self-reflective and self-awareness wondering challenge. In other words, it translates for the reader as, knowing what I have read and learned from, all of the above text, where do I go from here? How might I use that new understanding to decide whether and how to intervene in a dispute involving myself directly or as someone close to or responsible for others? Bringing that macro-level of analysis down to an actual dispute involvement, the question changes to, given what I have heard so far; what has just happened in the room; what has just been said by one or other of the disputants; how any of that is making me feel inside right now; may be challenging my efforts to be impartial or connecting with any bias, including my unconscious prejudicial bias, and potential judgementalism, what options are there for what to say, or do right now? Given the possibility of the intensity of these reflective questions it is worth remembering that at any point, a time-out break may be beneficial. Anecdotal evidence from practice shows that such breaks for refreshments, a short walk or smoke, frequently result in surprising movement in negotiations when the session is reconvened. It may be that this effect is the result of disputants taking time to reflect on how their behaviour and possible 'sticking to a position', may be approaching unreasonableness or unfairness.

That may in turn result in thoughts of more constructive proposals that might facilitate face-saving for self and others. Some providers find that time-out option so effective that they routinely build it into all sessions.

Reflective reading

A very useful reflective practice test when working in service delivery and helping services is, to what extent am I treating people with the care, positive regard, respect and quality, that I would expect to receive from them as their customer? Again, the reader may find it helpful here to take some time to note down some self-assessment questions at this stage. For example:

1. Knowing what I have learned so far from the reading, how far do I think I am going to be able to work in a way that demonstrates the qualities listed throughout the text?
2. What transferable skills might I be able to bring to such dispute resolution work from things that I do in my everyday work and life activity in problem-solving and helping people who may be having a hard time?
3. What particular qualities do I recognise as self-evident strengths, and which might I now need to develop further?

---

11 Some Important Cautionary Warnings to Bear in Mind

First, 'do no harm' – Work safely

Professional mediation practitioners usually see each disputant individually before deciding whether or not to offer mediation. Several matters have to be addressed at this meeting which are not necessary to describe here but of substantial importance is the matter of 'screening for safety'. Each person, including the mediator, must feel confident that as far as can be estimated, they feel safe to attend a joint meeting, with no foreseeable coercion, intimidation or risk of violence. The mediator must satisfy themselves that whether or not potential participants regard it as safe and want to go ahead, the ultimate decision on that rests with the practitioner. Anecdotal evidence showed that asking direct questions about risk, for example, regarding domestic violence does not necessarily result in disclosure nor do vague indirect lines of enquiry. As a consequence, both ends of that scale need to be addressed.

> The reader may find it helpful to consider and make some notes regarding what questions they consider might be helpful. What follows here are some tried and tested examples, that in principle should be asked equally of any participant where the LM is considering involvement in the dispute. At this stage, the reader might recap the earlier text on the use of questions in Chapter 6 and more examples will be given after completing this warnings list.

Whilst as initially stated, this book has kept theory to a minimum, in this section, it is important to include a summary of one theory studied in detail by professional mediators, that of human conflict and high emotion patterns with implications for safe practice. Skilled and experienced mediation practitioners learn how to read the signs of escalating emotion and its constructive management. Through this strategic process, they create conditions for calm reflective conversations. Even slowing down the pace of speech and a calm relaxed and open posture, facilitates an inner brain analysis by participants of their feelings and emotions. This internal discourse tends to result

DOI: 10.4324/9781003317005-11

in a more rational assessment of the risks to self and others if self-control is lost. In turn, this usually moves on to a memory scanning recall of similar past experiences of self or others about the socio-legal sanctions for violence to others. Practitioners also need to understand how the lower brain initiates a reaction – an 'autonomic' process initiated by the nerves located in the spinal column – that triggers chemicals which fuel the individuals responses to threats. In other words, the withdrawal of a hand from hot surfaces does not require analysis or instructions from the higher brain so it happens much faster. In this hormonal fight or flight reaction, adrenaline is produced to reinforce the capacity to stay and fight, whereas the strength to run away is facilitated by noradrenaline. Little is known about why some people produce more of one than the other, but it may be a combination of genetics, gender and social conditioning. The key issue for mediation and high conflict emotion management is that in the case of a 'fight fuel high', particularly in the male, it can take up to an hour or more for the effects to wear off, so it may well be wise to take a long break or postpone negotiations to another day. Such an incident should be carefully reviewed with all concerned, and options explored as to what needs to change to avoid any further risks, including the possible need to stop altogether and resort to alternatives such as professional dispute resolution.

Beware of unintentional consequences

As indicated earlier, the LM, whether personally involved as a disputant or responsible for the work of others, may consider offering to help resolve the conflict. In such a case, they will need to pay due regard to the potential risk of it at some point morphing into disciplinary or grievance procedures. More will be added on this issue later.

Take care to avoid potential legal consequences

In particular, caution needs to be exercised with ideas such as the recording of outcomes, and such terms as agreement. With professional mediation, details of conversations are regarded as 'Legally privileged', and as such cannot be used as evidence in any subsequent legal proceedings. Legal privilege belongs to the parties, not the practitioner, and as such can only be waived with the consent of both parties. The question that arises is to what extent would the outcome of any LM activity need to be recorded? Anecdotal experience in the early years of professional mediation practice found that not recording agreements often resulted in a breakdown of agreements. One possible explanation for this was that it may have involved one or another party, especially in the early stages of the process, deliberately failing to keep to all of the key parts of the plan. For example, where they still felt that any agreement did not yet include enough of their own outcome goals and expectations. Subsequent meetings would then involve spending time on differences in recollection of the fine details of dates and times. As a result of this time-consuming outcome, practitioners increasingly took to recording what was commonly termed 'outcome statements', either written on the day or posted to all within a few days. This quickly resulted in increasing numbers of hitherto agreements, now termed 'plans' being kept to since all involved in any meetings were aware that each had a written copy as an aide-memoir.

Some examples of impartial non-leading questions

These questions would normally be used by a practitioner not involved directly in a dispute. However, it is feasible that they could easily be used by people who are directly involved, in terms of jointly reviewing how they feel about each other, and the prospect of working together. Note again the open-question style throughout.

- What do you imagine it might feel like if you come to a joint mediation meeting with the other(s) involved?
- How easy or hard might it be for you to take a full part in the session?
- What might make it difficult to speak about what you want and need from such a meeting?
- How would you describe any arguments between you during recent weeks or months?
- How similar or different has that been to how it was before?
- When you disagree, what does it sound like or look like, and how does it usually end up?
- When you argue, does the same person always win, or might it go either way?
- What happens if someone begins to get so angry that they look like they might find it hard to control their temper?
- What sort of things might trigger such anger during an argument between you?
- When things get heated has anything been damaged or broken?
- What was the worst ever ending to such an argument?
- Has anybody ever hit anyone, or been hit, and if so, what sort of injury resulted? Was it treated by a doctor?

Some examples of circular questions

- Might the other person(s) say they are frightened of or intimidated by you?
- Might they feel you are frightened of or intimidated by them?
- How comfortable would you imagine the other(s) might feel about sitting in the same room as you?
- How worried or concerned might they be about things you say or do in a joint meeting?

Making the process as constructive as possible

Substantial anecdotal experience over many years as a professional mediator showed that several principles were consistently associated with positive
outcomes and settlements. As such, it may be reasonable to suppose that
these principles might also work effectively if used by the untrained LM if
shared with all involved at the early stages of exploring possible meetings.
It is not envisaged that they would constitute or take the form of a con-
tractual or possibly legal agreement, nor be signed. They are simply a set
of ideas that might look to be fair and reasonable to bear in mind during
the process. A useful way for the LM to introduce this idea might be to say
that what they have learned from their reading is that mediators often ask,
would it help you all to know what mediators have learned from experience,
helps to keep discussions effective and productive? When they ask that,
the response is, in most instances, affirmative and hence, what can then be
shared is the following:

  Mediation works best when all those involved in the meetings

1. Take turns to speak and do not interrupt each other.
2. Call each other by first names, not 'he' or 'she' or indeed more pejora-
   tive labels.
3. Use 'I' statements – for example not 'he/she is always letting me down
   and hurting me' but 'I feel hurt or let down when certain things happen'.
4. Try to describe what we want, rather than what we don't want. For
   example, what we would like other people to do differently in future,
   rather than what we don't want them to do.
5. Try to avoid blaming or attacking others, or engaging in put-downs, and
   instead try to ask questions of each other to clarify and understand them.
6. Try to avoid making rigid demands or taking fixed positions and
   instead, express ourselves in terms of our personal needs and interests,
   and the outcomes that we hope to achieve.
7. Listen carefully when any one person is speaking and avoid reacting by
   interrupting them.
8. Listen carefully and with an open mind to try to understand each other's
   needs and interests.
9. Recognise that, even if we do not agree with each other, each of us is
   entitled to our own views and perspectives. A constructive outcome
   arrangement does not in itself require that such opinions are required
   to change.
10. Try to avoid dwelling on things that did not work in the past, or what
    people did wrongly or badly, but instead, try to focus on how things
    might be done differently in the future.
11. Attempt to avoid unproductive arguing or expressing high emotion and
    anger about the past, and try instead to use the time in mediation to
    work towards the fairest and most constructive agreement possible.

12. Be able to speak up if we feel that something about the mediation process or meeting is not working for us.
13. Express our concerns if we feel that anyone is not being reasonable or open-minded.
14. Feel able to ask to take a break when we need to.
15. Think about what, if any, more specific and personal principles that are not listed above, we may want to be added to the list.

These principles are aspirational and should be openly acknowledged as such by all involved. Principles do not ensure a panacea or prevent the expression of natural emotions associated with disputes. The content of this list of principles must be acceptable to all involved and should include scope for more potential bespoke and individual additions. Strategically they could be talked through in the first exploratory pre-mediation meetings and participants be encouraged to take them away, consider them in detail, and come to a future meeting with thoughts about how useful they are and with any additional principles they might wish to add.

Reflective reading

The above text raises several potentially challenging issues that may have raised concerns for the LM. Consequently, this may be an appropriate moment to reflect on the extent to which such matters feel manageable, and if not, what steps the LM can take to reduce any negative consequences arising. Attempts to apply any level of social scientific objectivity and analysis are always of value for practitioners. Nevertheless, professional anecdotal experience tends to confirm that intuitive and 'gut-level' senses are always worthy of reflection and may well lead to a decision to not engage in a dispute. The College of Mediators Code of Practice, under the heading of 'Voluntary participation' includes the clear advice 'Any participant or mediator is free to withdraw at any time'. The familiar maxim 'better to be safe than sorry' has its valid place here.

---

12 Buying What We Sell Matters

To What Extent Do Mediators Apply Their Principles and Professional Expertise to the Management of Conflict in Their Own Daily Lives?

The following was originally published in English in the Revista de Mediacion Journal Vol 8 N0. (2015), and in Spanish in the same edition. An edited version has also been included as a chapter in Mediation and Dispute Resolution: Contemporary Issues and Developments (Whatling, 2021, Chapter 10). Both have been adapted and reduced for reproduction here.

Given that the focus of this book is centred on empowering the LM it would seem only fair and reasonable to add some comments based on anecdotal experience of how far trained practitioners 'practice what they preach'.

'The cobbler's children have no shoes' – the essence of this maxim is to describe the phenomenon whereby certain professionals are so busy with work for their customers that they neglect to use their skills to help themselves in their daily life and work.

For example, the electrician who never finishes the wiring in their own house, the web designer that hasn't finished their website, or the physician who neglects their health.

This section will raise issues about the extent to which mediators, as experts in conflict resolution, can apply their everyday 'bread and butter' skills and strategies to conflicts that arise in their daily lives.

In particular, it will:

- Identify the problems that we all know exist, to a greater or lesser degree, namely that in all families and organisations, conflict is inevitable – and that it is just as common within mediation organisations.
- Raise awareness as to the extent of the problem.
- Identify some common characteristics of the problem.
- Remind readers of the everyday professional methods of dispute resolution management of such issues.
- Offer some ideas for how such personal disputes might be managed.

The last three decades of the development of mediation in the UK have witnessed conflicts between professional mediation colleagues that have been perplexing and at times potentially very serious.

DOI: 10.4324/9781003317005-12

The conflicts arising from these disputes have had all of the ingredients of potentially destructive conflict – the early history; the trigger; the spark; the fanning of the flames; and finally, in some cases, the metaphorical destructive impact on relationships.

Such processes are all too familiar to mediators in their daily work with parties in dispute. Throughout a few weeks or months conflict narratives are written, line by line and paragraph by paragraph, into chapters that are to become the history books, or so-called 'truths' and facts. As every mediator knows, each person's dispute 'history' records a very different account of what had led up to the rifts.

Each disputants friends and family members rally to take their side in support, as the voices of the so-called 'Greek chorus' swell to amplify and further embroider the historical accounts as described by one author: When the mediator first meets with the disputants each person has a story to tell. These stories consist of three parts – a version of the events, a complaint about the other, and a problem definition. Each version is designed by each disputant to show the mediator how good they are and how each is the victim of the situation. Conversely, the second part, the complaint, is designed to show the mediator how bad the other is. The key hallmark of the definition of the problem is that each person defines it in such a way that it can only be solved by a change in the behaviour or position of the other.

Conflict in social and organisational environments is inevitable and inescapable. It is not a question of *if* a conflict exists but how well it is managed that matters. We also know that without conflict there would be very little change for the better, or improvement in most aspects of life. Or as one writer expresses it, conflict can signal constructive ways of bringing about change and of re-ordering lives. At least the potential for positive change is greater when there is anger than where there is the helplessness and hopelessness of depression (Roberts, 2008, p. 108). We can also all be involved in sorting out many everyday personal disputes, without the process necessarily escalating into conflict. Sadly, such conflicts continue to this day to occur in mediation organisations, despite many years of developing an understanding of how to manage them constructively.

These conflicts can have potentially very serious consequences for individuals, the organisations concerned, and potentially innocent bystanders, within the wider professional arena.

Commonly, such disputes are often 'dissolved' rather than 'resolved' – for example by one side-stepping down or leaving – a consequence of which is that those unresolved feelings subsequently tend to resurface in any future conflict in the organisation.

But it's different when we are personally involved isn't it?

We may understand what people mean when they say that, but no, it should not be different. Mediators open their doors to the public as experts in conflict management and dispute resolution, and should therefore quite reasonably be expected to manage it constructively when it involves them personally.

It is all the more imperative that mediators 'practice what they preach' – 'put their money where their mouth is' – or indeed to be able 'to buy that which they sell'.

So what then can be done? Some ideas for managing the conflicts.

What follows is little more than a reminder of what mediators already know and use in practice and a checklist of potential options available to them:

Andrew Floyer Acland describes what is known as the 'PIN' (Positions, Interests, Needs) diagram (see more on this in Chapter 13). The three levels of the pyramid diagram show how at the peak are the positions that disputants take and typically bring to mediation. The second level relates to wants, values and interests and the third level to the deeper needs of all parties to the dispute. Like the iceberg, the tip, or peak, is often all that is observable above the surface in the initial stages of mediation.

Through skilful needs-led questions, the practitioner gradually facilitates a move away from each disputants opening positional statements, and so exposes the common areas of interest and needs of each party. As each new pyramid sub-level emerges, joint areas of common values and interests are uncovered – and more important still at the lower level, the crucial area of joint needs are revealed. For example, when directors and managers attempt to impose new contracts of employment terms and conditions, often without prior consultation with those who are directly affected by the changes, each side tends to quickly assume 'positions'.

Typically these positions include positional statements by employers such as, sign the new contracts now or face immediate dismissal, perhaps adding some moral pressure by citing the potentially serious financial consequences for the organisation unless the contracts are accepted. On the staff side, the responses are commonly along the lines of, impose those contracts and we will have no option but to withdraw our labour. Before very long, such opening position statements tend to degenerate into even greater threats.

However experienced we are as practitioners we may all still be as capable as any other human being, of getting drawn into interpersonal conflict. This occurs through a natural 'fight-flight' threat inclination, often driven by a fear of loss, so we may adopt a rigid position, make threats, and begin to metaphorically write our idiosyncratic historical narrative of the what, who and how of the dispute. However, what has hopefully changed over the years of involvement in dispute resolution, is that after a few days or weeks of such behaviour, the practitioner will hear a little inner voice that goes something like, hang on, you know very well what is going on here and what you are you doing, you are stoking the fire and fanning the flames. What this situation needs instead is for you to initiate a dialogue in which you ask the significant other(s) to talk about their wants, needs and fears, and ask in return that they will listen to yours. From such internal challenges will hopefully flow constructive ideas as to how to resolve the dispute, and re-establish good working relationships to the mutual benefit of all concerned. Given that this was originally published for trained, qualified and experienced mediators, so hopefully it will be of some value to an LM if and when they find themselves in similar personal situations:

1. Remember that to be the LM, you must believe that the majority of people in dispute are capable of being a) reasonable and b) rational. The problem is that when they first come they are often behaving in ways that are very unreasonable and irrational.
2. Use your primary communication organs proportionately – two ears, two eyes and one mouth – so do more listening and observing than speaking – 'Wise men speak because they have something to say; Fools because they have to say something', Plato.
3. Never press the email or text 'send' button till you have slept on it and be aware of the damage that modern electronic cryptic communications create in today's social, personal and professional world.
4. Resist at all costs the temptation to make threats. When we do that it is usually a signal of desperation, and we are frequently not in a position to carry them through – not least without financial costs. As a generalisation, people in a weak position make threats, people in strong positions don't threaten, they just act.
5. Remember to reframe the dispute and potential crisis as an opportunity for change and transformation, towards better understanding and the greater good, health and well-being of organisations and professional colleagues.
6. Don't resort to the old 'personality clash' cop-out – a commonly used explanation by disputants to account for problems – and yet how hard it is to resist sometimes. The author in his early days of practice had a team colleague with who, from frequent conversations and periodic arguments in team meetings, appeared to have little in common. Both seemed to be aware that their core values about people appeared to be so far at odds, that they managed to avoid co-working together for over a year. This avoidance appeared to come from concern that such differences would inevitably be demonstrated to clients during the co-working working partnership. Eventually, it became clear that this avoidant behaviour was having a negative impact on the rest of the team. Discovering this, they eventually agreed to discuss it and as a result, they agreed to work on a case together. In reality, they worked together very effectively and continued to do so from then on, with no demonstrable evidence of any of the conflicts of values hitherto feared.
7. In referring to this problem, Acland affirms these actions when he writes, the only way I know of actually resolving a personality clash is head-on: by admitting the feeling and setting out to trace its causes. If this is done fully and honestly, looking at each other's: values, opinions,

assumptions about each other, prejudices about the background, education, even accent or race, then maybe the situation can be redeemed (Acland, 1990, p. 61).

8. It may help to agree on some statements of principles against which to evaluate outcome agreements – for example, a mutual commitment to early win/win settlements and a return to former constructive and productive working relationships.

9. Try to avoid the natural human temptation to engage in the psychological defence mechanism of 'displacement'. We are all bound to want to protect our own private, (internal), and public, (external), self-image or 'face'. When the mediator hears a client say, I know I wasn't always the ideal spouse/boss/business partner, they know only too well, that the next word will be a resounding 'BUT', usually followed by a long list of the sins and failings of the other. To resist doing so is hard, since if we accept even 50% of the blame or responsibility for what has gone wrong, we may still find that hard to live with, because of its negative impact on our self-image.

10. Why beholdest thou the mote that is in thy brother's eye, but considerest not the beam that is in thine own eye? [Matthew 7:3]. Or as one writer puts it: Conflict provides opportunities for people to express aspects of their personality which are normally kept hidden. More than this, people project on to others their own personality or behaviour: they accuse other people of doing things or behaving in ways in which they themselves are behaving, or want to behave (Acland, 1990, p. 105).

11. Ask for help from trusted colleagues, ideally who are known to all sides as capable of being objective and impartial.

12. Don't react or retaliate. A friend going through divorce used to read the latest inflammatory and goading letter from his wife's solicitor − and then his own equally adversarial response. Several times it was pointed out that by far the best way to end this war of words was not to react – since nothing annoys our enemies more than refusing to retaliate. His response was inevitably that he just could not resist it. He admitted that he was enjoying the adrenalin rush and ritual of this 'game', despite the potential damaging side-effect it might have on his future relationship with his children.

13. Remember that win-win is not just the absence of win-lose or lose-lose, but an outcome where the 'total result of the outcome can be greater than the sum of its parts'. In other words, by engaging in constructive option development, we may well discover outcomes that are better for all concerned, including organisations, than either side had previously anticipated.

14. Reward your achievements by celebrating with the other person(s), perhaps with mutual friends and colleagues. By your example of personal and professional maturity, you may well be an inspiration to others when they encounter similar conflicts.

What is striking about these proposals is that they can be usefully summed up as a reflection of the biblical exhortation – do unto others as you would have them do unto you. The hope is that mediators everywhere, in the best interests of reflective practice, will reflect on this chapter and continue to reflect on the key issue – what is it that, as experts in our field and craft, makes it so difficult for us to routinely practice what we preach?

13 Some Illuminative Case Examples from Different Dispute Contexts

To protect the identity of real people, these case studies are fictionalised. However, they are taken from a mixture and assortment of real-life examples. The reader might like to imagine how they might intervene in each scenario and in particular what sort of questions they might use with the disputants individually and in any joint meetings. The following examples will include various dispute contexts including neighbours, family and workplace.

The case of the elderly lady with the snappy dog and the loud music player neighbour. Grace, an elderly widow lived in a small ground-floor housing association flat with her aged Jack Russell Sam. Tim, a 25-year-old medical student lived alone in the flat above, each sharing a communal entrance door. They also shared a small front garden with a gate. Both had made a complaint about the other, starting with Grace who objected to Tim frequently playing loud music late at night which kept her and Sam awake. Tim meantime, when contacted by the association officer complained that the dog would meet him at the gate barking loudly and, following him along the path, would persistently snap at his ankles, and the bottoms of his jeans. Both spoke of how their friends supported them totally, taking sides, progressively 'embroidering' their case, and offering suggestions based on what they would do if in that situation, including making threats based on potential breaches of tenancy, and even legal action. Apart from some occasional brief shouting between them, neither had attempted any problem-solving conversations. As a would-be LM, how might the reader consider intervening? The picture so far is presented as a fairly typical community neighbour dispute with all the potential of escalating to a higher level of conflict. The visiting housing officer tended to listen to each complainant and make suggestions as to resolving the issues. Examples of these were that Grace should keep her pet in when she knew Tim was due home, fit Sam with a muzzle and perhaps use earplugs. Tim had a very similar meeting in which it was suggested that he should use headphones or turn the sound down low at a mutually agreed hour in the evening. A similar warning was made to each regarding a potential breach of tenancy regulations. At his stage, typically a trained community mediation practitioner might offer a meeting, initially with each disputant

DOI: 10.4324/9781003317005-13

individually. In particular, unlike the housing department, they might wonder how to define this problem. In other words, is this a problem caused by the disputants as people, or of one of heel snapping dogs and loud music? The distinction is potentially crucial to how any problem-solving activity may be attempted. The snappy dog and loud music have intervened in a neighbourly relationship, in a sense, the two elements have become imposed on the two people. Consequently, this is where negotiations need to be focused, not on the neighbours as people but the external factors. Hence, with such a switch of mindset and problem definition, we can begin to intervene in such a style that is typically described as being hard on the problem and soft on the people. If, as suggested, we regard dogs and noise as problems imposed in a place or situation where they are not wanted or are considered disruptive, we can set about helping the disputants to self-determine options for removing them. The next strategic move is to use a style of questioning that digs deeper into the meanings of dogs and music to the people concerned. Typically, a suitable question to Grace might be something like, help me understand more about the importance of Sam to you. What does he mean to your daily life and how long it has been like that. It is interesting to note that the 'help me understand' question tends to work well with disputants since the underlying meta-communication is that it is the interest of the client to enhance the helper's understanding and hence to be best able to help. Combined with that effect is a subconscious power balancing dynamic that is about a help seeker feeling good when asked to help a helper. In the interests of even-handedness, the same line of enquiry would be used with Tim. The typical response from Grace would probably involve such as, that Sam was everything to her whole life, ever since she and her late husband found him in a refuge and grew to love him more every day as he did them. They never went anywhere without him and he followed one or other of them everywhere. He sits with her when watching TV and sleeps on her feet in bed. He had become even more special to her since after 50 years of marriage her husband passed away. She found it impossible to imagine how she could have survived that grief without Sam because apart from anything else, she still needed to get out of bed and take care of him. Even though sometimes she found it hard to get herself up and dressed to go out, except that she knew he needed the exercise. What happens a lot when she does, is that people often stop to chat, particularly other dog walkers, so she met people socially in a way that would never happen were she indoors all day. Her two children were married, one living abroad and the other very long distance from her so she rarely sees them. Consequently, she talks to Sam all day about all sorts of things, especially about her late hubby, and it was almost as if he understands what she is going on about. Finally, she probably speaks about how Tim's periodic parties with his several friends also tend to finish late and so makes it hard for her to sleep as well as upsetting her dog.

OK, so what about Tim? A potential LM may be wondering, how they could follow that? As an anecdotal aside, one mediator colleague used to argue that she was hopeless at seeing both parties. And hence would see one, with a colleague seeing the other, then conferring together before a joint meeting. Her reason for this was that having seen the first person she totally believed their story and version of events and hence could not be impartial if seeing the other at a solo assessment. Most colleagues views were different since typically, they too would tend to find the first eminently believable and perhaps wonder how someone could have lived with such an awful person and situation for so long. They would then find that they had the same response to the other. This healthy cognitive dissonance effect inevitably enabled them to experience that the truth was somewhere in between both. Whilst on the subject of truth, it is worth commenting here that the search for the truth in dispute resolution is a 'fool's errand'. If such a goal is regarded as key then it is probably best pursued in a Court of law. Here too sadly, any such determination and judgement are frequently a result of the skills levels of lawyers and barristers often combined with the idiosyncratic values of the Judge on the day. In mediation, what are called truths or facts are in reality usually more 'perceptions of realty' and not, as often perceived as trickery or attempts to deceive. When mediation works well, it facilitates and empowers people to unpack their stories and reformat them into more balanced realities. Moving between disputants individually requires doing the best to set aside any potential stereotypes or prejudices, including 'unconscious bias' that may have had significant perception, power and control, over constructive interpersonal communication. A key issue here is that whatever potential assumptions may have been implanted in the mind after the first solo meeting, must metaphorically be moved to a different space in the brain. The second person has a right to start with a clean sheet, including at this stage any potential risk allegations from the first person(s). Those will have to be raised at some stage, but to start there is to risk negatively positioning the second person. In the early stages of mediation, disputants were usually seen in a joint session from the start. There were several problems arising from this. In particular, in a highly emotional situation, it was often difficult to allow each person to tell their story without frequent defensive interruptions from the other. It also became clear that it took significantly longer to manage the process than with the solo meeting. What was also discovered was that whichever person went first, almost always 'negatively positioned the other'. In other words, some-what akin to chess or tennis, given two equally skilled players, the one to go first inevitably starts with a move or serve advantage, and indeed may win that game. So too it is with the joint first meeting, the second speaker is commonly unable to tell their story purely but will frequently intersperse it with defensive references to the first. So, returning to Tim and starting with the same style of question used with Grace, he might be encouraged to describe what his particular music and periodic parties with mates meant in his life. Tim's position may be that he is a student nurse working shifts in a hospital accident and emergency department. The hours are long, staff shortages are acute and the stress at times is almost unbearable. When at its worst, he is frequently minded to give it up and find less stressful work. However, deep down he always wanted to be a doctor, but having failed to get good enough A levels, nursing seemed a good alternative. It was also conceivable that over time he could study and retake his A levels. He had met doctors who managed that and had talked of the benefits of their nursing and patient care experience to later medical studies. The worst shifts were the late ones where A&E patients arrived with life-changing or fatal injuries or major organ malfunctions. All too often they were either not going to make it through the night, or would be permanently incapacitated mentally or physically. The collective team effect on morale and sense of incompetence, however unjustified, combined with managing the expectations, fears and disbelief of relatives, at the inability of doctors to save their loved ones. Combined with cases of suicide, self-harm, and substance abuse they all added up to be the worst nights to come home alone and to clear the mind. There were times too when Tim had no choice but to complete study assignments. His music was the only reliable option in bringing him down from the potentially overwhelming emotion, and risk of post-traumatic stress, to the extent that it enabled him to study and complete assignments. There were similar positive effects from his periodic parties, especially with those from work experiencing similar stress levels. Hopefully, the reader is following the difference of style here between what is known as 'directive mediation', possibly as may be tried by housing officers – and note the links too with TA theory earlier – in particular critical or controlling parent ego states. Typically a housing officer may tell each disputant what they should do in future to resolve the problem, for example, lock the dog in and stop loud music after 10 pm. Such a style would usually be followed up by a caution, probably in writing, that if either fails to make such changes they may well find themselves in breach of tenancy regulations and risk eviction. The next level down from the directive style is what is known as 'evaluative, or normative mediation', in which people are advised as to what commonly happens in similar disputes. The message here is based on an attempt to move the dispute in the direction of options based on other cases, with a clear inference that they would be wise to save time, costs, risk of eviction and further escalation by following a similar path to resolution. Both of the above possibilities may appeal to the disputants as a 'quick-fix' solution, and yet leave no sense of client-centred fairness, empowerment or specific connection to their own needs as uncovered by the 'facilitative style' demonstrated by the above solo meetings with Grace and Tim. From this facilitative approach, it can be argued that 'How goes the pre-mediation assessment meeting is how goes the mediation'. Whilst a longer time commitment may have resource implications for some, this is commonly rebalanced by the speed at which negotiations can progress, compared with the alternative high 'conflict saturated stories', and emotion in joint assess-ments. In short, the work done with developing a deeper understanding of the needs of Grace and Tim will in all probability result in a more empathic exchange of potential win-win options. Typically, the 'telling of the stories' in one-one meetings results in the forming of a special rela-tionship between each person and the helper. This relationship is such that disputants are usually keen to demonstrate to a practitioner their wish to be seen as reasonable and rational people. There are choices as to how to start a joint meeting and the disputants can be invited to consider their preferences. One option is for each person to tell their story them-selves; another is for both to agree that the practitioner summarises the stories on their behalf. With summaries, it is really important to do this directly to the person concerned, rather than to the other, as though in the style of a translation. In this case, both responded with a respectful acknowledgement of the reality of the other's situation and the deeper meanings of the dog to Grace and music to Tim. Not uncommonly, each will at this point express some regret to the other for their past behaviour and the problems it caused. Moving on to the stage of options develop-ment and with suggestions from each, in this instance, the proposed set-tlement was soon determined. Grace, whose sitting room overlooked the front gate, would keep Sam in until Tim had gone indoors. Tim in turn agreed to update Grace, by a note through her door, of any shift changes or other events affecting his return time. As to the music, Tim might agree to turn it down every night by 10 pm, which was Grace's usual bed-time. He had already discovered that it was possible to buy cordless headphones, which meant that he would be free to move around the flat as well as play his music. Tim agreed to be sure to turn the music down low by 10 pm when occasionally entertaining his friends. It should be noted that the choice of venue for a joint meeting may have potential power balance implications, and so will usually take place at a neutral venue. In this instance, Tim had no concerns about it being in Grace's flat, and that saved her having to travel to a venue. An unexpected bonus that took everyone by surprise was that after some initial barking, Sam moved progressively closer to Tim, who responded by stroking him and eventually allowing Sam to climb up to sit beside him. The involvement of pets is relatively rare and yet where it does happen, it has been found that it can have a positive effect on participants. In this instance, it was as if Sam sensed that, by being in the same room together, Tim posed no threat to Grace. In a routine follow-up review, it transpired that para-doxically it had reached the point where Sam was allowed to greet Tim at the gate on his return from work. It had also moved on to the point where the relationship between Grace and Tim progressed to the point where she would bake cakes and biscuits and invite him in for tea at weekends – as though providing a surrogate son or grandson for her. Tim for his part became a reassuring and supportive carer presence at times when grace was occasionally concerned about her health. All of these bonus outcomes reflect the earlier references to win-win outcomes described by Fisher and Ury. In other words, they represent unforeseen serendipitous benefits and so demonstrate again that a win-win is greater than the sum of the parts.

A family case study – Family ghosts

Steve and Kay were attending mediation to resolve issues regarding contact arrangements for their two children, Tanya, seven, and Sam, eight. In mediation, both presented as pleasant low-conflict people, with a mutual sense of sadness at the end of their marriage. It took four sessions to reach an agreement, and, in the last few minutes of every one Kay, would become very tearful. Each time when asked, she declined to say what was making her so upset until the final meeting. She explained that her parents had divorced when she was seven, the same age as Tanya. From that point on, as a child, at every contact visit, each parent 'grilled' her for detailed information about the other. They also made her carry angry and inflammatory letters to and from between them. She had found that so very upsetting it left her wishing she did not have to continue the contact arrangement. As the tears flowed, she said that here she was now an adult, married with two children, and yet her parents were still doing that to her to this day. At this point, she pointed at Steve and said that he too had 'history'. Steve explained that his parents had also divorced when he was seven and, allegedly on the grounds of his mother's objection to contact, he never saw his father again. After he had married, Kay encouraged him to try to find his dad. It took over a year until, with the help of the Salvation Army, he found and was reunited with his dad. His dad was thrilled to be back in contact and to spend time with his grandchildren. One year later he died of cancer. The reader might like to consider for a moment what, if anything, they might have said to Kay and Steve at that moment, in the silence that followed. The mediator struggled to think of what to say. Eventually, he commented that it was really hard to think of what to say. However, what had become very clear was that each of them knew better than any expert in the world, about what their children need from them now and in the future. That in turn meant that they could use that experience and understanding to decide together how to do it wisely and well. Alternatively, they could do what their parents did to them. Knowing them from the meetings and how much they cared about and loved them, it seemed highly probable that they would make the right decisions. They were reminded that should they have any problems implementing the plans, they knew how to make contact again and how mediation worked, so they could always come back. The tears stopped. Kay hugged the mediator and Steve shook hands warmly, saying 'Thanks, mate'. In conclusion, is it feasible that the LM could also have helped here. Perhaps a good mutually trusted and dependable family member, or good friend, could have helped resolve this sad situation. It is worth reflecting that, alongside the progressive development of dispute resolution and legal services, the probability is that very many similar disputes are being resolved worldwide every day, by people themselves, with help from relatives, friends, faith and community leaders. We simply do not know statistically how many manage to do that without professional interventions. It is also likely that pre-industrial close-knit family and community networks were much more involved and supportive in such matters.

An unsuccessful family mediation example

Sally and her partner Kevin had been separated for some six months, their children Zak aged six and Sara aged four living with their mother in the family home. Sally claimed that Kevin had an affair with a married friend Tanya, which he denied, claiming that they were just good friends and work colleagues. The primary dispute was over contact arrangements between Kevin and the children. They had never tried mediation but, encouraged by Sally's lawyer, had applied to the courts for a contact order. The latter order typically specified staying contact with Kevin every other weekend, alternating birthdays and public holidays with an agreed share arrangement for school holidays, to fit with his work schedule. Despite the Court order, contact was constantly disrupted and often prevented by Sally, who alleged that the children were not safe with their dad. Examples were that she alleged that his car seat belts were second hand and substandard and declined to share the ones fitted to her car. On another, he had left an upstairs window open in his flat whilst fresh paint dried, which meant the children could have climbed out. There were very frequent return visits to legal advisors and the Court, where Sally was ordered again to comply with the order. It was finally also proposed that they should be referred by their Lawyers to mediation. Strictly speaking, the Court cannot order mediation, since disputants cannot be forced to mediate. In the UK, attempts have been made in the past and seem likely to continue, to make it mandatory, as is increasingly so with binding arbitration. References to mediation in the UK continue to be very varied, some are made by self-referral or encouraged by the legal advisors, where disputants started by consulting with them. Compared with the picture some three decades ago many more Lawyers are inclined to recommend it before resorting to the Courts. Indeed many lawyers over that period have themselves trained as mediators. The result of its historical evolution has led to a situation whereby some disputants may still join the Courts route first, often unaware of other options. Where that happens there are anecdotally two key impacts on disputants compared with the mediation route option. Firstly, they, like others involved in the legal context, may discover that the experience leaves themselves, advisers and courts, somewhat exasperated and failing to resolve matters. This also tends to reflect the fact that whilst a Court can deal with presented facts, it will not deal with disputants emotions. The impact of that will quite often make disputants regard the dispute resolution process as offering new hope, that, with some help, they may be able to resolve matters themselves. Unfortunately, another less constructive effect of starting with the court route may arise as a consequence of how legal advisors have in effect, 'trained' clients to provide pieces of evidence against each other, with which to empower their advisor to defeat the other side. In such cases, it can often take a whole first joint mediation session or more, to re-educate the disputants into a needs-led discourse. It is often said that mediation is an educative activity, insofar as people in disputes and feeling that a solution is impossible, are gradually re-empowered and learn that they can, with help, resolve it themselves. This 'transformative' experience will ideally equip them to use that learning in any future disputes they become involved in. Sadly, Kevin and Sally, after four meetings of highly skilled mediation, demonstrated a total inability to understand this difference and make the transitional shift. They were reminded constantly about the pointlessness of bringing pieces of evidence since it was not the role of the practitioner to determine who was right or wrong, nor to form a judgement. Eventually, the mediator reluctantly ended the meetings and referred them back to their lawyers. It was also suggested that a referral be made to the Children and Family Courts Advisory and Support Service, (CAFCASS) – formerly the Family Courts Welfare Service – staffed by probation officers. This process involves all those involved being interviewed, including the children, and the allocated officer making a report with a recommendation to the Court. A significant difference here is that, unlike mediators who are professionally accountable to the disputants, CAFCASS staff are directly accountable to the Court. Here yet again, some mutually trusted friend might have had enough influence to be able to intervene as LM.

A workplace dispute

Jenny aged 60 and Dave 25 were co-workers in the finance office of an engineering company and were responsible for all invoicing and payment processes. They had worked together for some five years, most of which time being characterised by a friendly and humorous rapport. They had generally managed their responsibilities well, despite some periods of high stress caused by other departments and customers, when accounting systems were not properly followed. Jenny had played an important role in mentoring Dave into their role, responsibilities, financial systems and ever-increasing workload. Dave who had no experience in similar work, had struggled to adapt, and so appreciated her support. For her part, Jenny with no children of her own had enjoyed something of a quasi-maternal role. What triggered the dispute was when a highly stressful event cropped up, affected to a large measure by an outdated financial software system, the firm came close to substantial losses of a new contract and income. The company boss Trev called Jenny into his office and expressed considerable frustration, primarily aimed at her as the senior worker and de facto 'finance office manager'. Jenny duly protested, because the roots of the problem lay with the outdated finance system and also that she was not the only staff member in that office. The boss, renowned for 'having a short fuse' declared firstly, that from then on she was formally designated as the finance office manager. Secondly, he wanted the matter sorted out quickly and in a way that would appease the new customer, for example, by receiving an apology from her. Finally, he considered that she should deal with software issues, about which he knew nothing, at whatever the cost, and update him when all such issues were resolved. He added that unless she made all of that happen 'heads may have to roll', and their jobs replaced by staff who would do better. Jenny's reporting back to Dave resulted in an instantly negative reaction based on her sudden promotion when he had always believed them to be equals. He was far from sure that he could continue to work under such an arrangement especially given the threat of job losses. Uncertain as to what to do, jenny conferred with their union rep with whom she had a good professional relationship based on previous disputes with staff in other departments. Steve, the union rep had fortunately attended, a workshop on dispute resolution awareness training. At a joint meeting, he listened well to Jenny and Dave's version of events. He then embarked on a list of needs-led questioning and explored a deeper level of the practical issues regarding their roles and financial systems problems. Having summarised to the satisfaction of both, Steve then commented that it seemed clear to him that the problems were not primarily centred on their relationship, but the shortcomings of seriously outdated and inadequate financial systems. It had also become obvious that the two people who knew better about these issues than anyone else in the company were themselves. He wondered if there was any mileage in the two of them doing a detailed analysis of the system and identifying the weak points in the whole process from early engineering quotations, through contracting agreements, to signing off payments. The response from Jenny and Dave was generally positive and yet they were in doubt as to how much work would be involved in analysing the systems, given how overworked and stressed they were already, by having to sort out the everyday consequences of failing systems. With Steve's help, they set about estimating and costing how much overtime would be involved and exploring ball-park estimates for modern software systems, including a cost-benefit analysis of each option. Steve appreciated that knowing Trev as well he did, he would be prepared to put the plan to him on their behalf. Somewhat predictably Trev responded by repeating that all he was interested in was getting a fast solution to the problem and an end to the bickering between Jenny and Dave. He also agreed with initial overtime costing limits, to be reviewed only on receiving an update report on progress. A series of paid overtime dates were soon agreed upon. Here we see another example of positive reframing of the problem from risks of loss of employment to optimism based on a constructive problem-solving plan. It also highlights the benefits of focussing the problem on financial systems rather than bickering workers – the former was the problem, not the people. Yet again, a serendipitous benefit was to draw the two key workers closer together in the interests of cooperative and constructive problem solving and saving their jobs. The outcome would potentially not only solve the problem for Trev with minimal effort on his part but also save the loss of two key workers and the costs involved in replacing them. The relatively low-key and benign involvement of the union rep also helped avoid the risk of industrial action, arising from disciplinary and grievance procedures, as well as costly time-consuming employment tribunal hearings. The plan worked better than any of the participants could have imagined. Dave and Jenny carried out a detailed analysis of the accounting system problems both from software and other departments' periodic failures. A couple of weekend overtime days proved to be enough to put together a report both on problems and solutions including costings for the best software options. The boss was duly impressed and authorised the software expenditure. He also authorised Jane and Dave to hold meetings with heads of other departments linked to the financial system at different stages, to clarify what each was required to do to keep the system working well.

Uncovering mutual needs

A particularly useful model for the analysis of such disputes is what is known as the 'PIN' diagram, (Figure 13.1), (Reproduced from 'Resolving Disputes Without Going to Court' Andrew Ackland (1995)).

In the early stages of a dispute, it is common for those involved to communicate from their positions sometimes referred to as 'being in their positions'. This activity is akin to the top of the pyramids being like the tips of icebergs with the next two levels being submerged. Typically such communications are characterised by threats and counter threats from an assumption that the other side will be sufficiently intimidated to give in. In reality, it commonly has the opposite effect and helps to escalate what started as a dispute into a conflict. For example, the workers and their union reps may demand wage increases and longer holidays, which if not forthcoming is likely to result in strike action and production losses. Typically, the bosses duly respond with threats of sackings and loss of wages. The task of the practitioner is, by the use of strategic questions, to explore with all involved, their interests, values, wants, and future aspirations, which may have some common ground between both sides that might be negotiable. However, at the lowest level of the triangle, shared needs are much more fundamental and crucial to explore and draw into a mutual negotiation discourse. In the process, they should minimise the need to threaten and bully either side into submission. One consequence of a failed negotiation and constructive settlement is that one side may 'lose the battle' but not 'the war'. As a consequence,

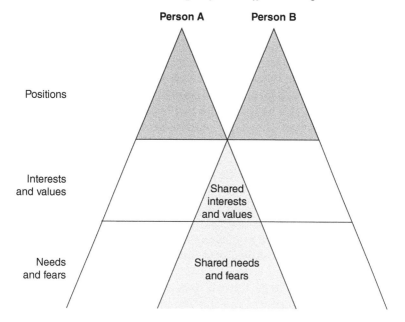

Figure 13.1 PIN diagram.

they will look at any future disputes, not just in terms of the new issues, but for potential 'ad-ons', in the hope of compensation in the next settlement. History shows many examples such as coal miners versus pit owners. Every new dispute carried with it a sense of duty to remedy the losses and perceived oppression, of previous generations of pit workers. In the case referred to above, respectful explorations of needs and fears will typically reveal common comparable ground such as the workers need to earn wages to support their family, together with a need for a predictable secure tenure of employment. The employer, on the other hand, needs predictable and continuing improvements in productivity, quality assurance and financial growth. The larger the company and its involvement of shareholders, the greater the risks of being unable to replace an entire trained workforce, and hence the risk of liquidation. Some of the most successful outcomes of such disputes have resulted in not just a settlement, but a win-win as described earlier, namely that both sides are helped to identify not just an agreement, but hitherto hidden added benefits. For example, through constructive and imaginative option developments, in return for agreed improved salary and extra holiday days, increased productivity and improved product quality, the workers gain shares in the company and profits bonuses. Other innovations such as regular 'quality' circle meetings between bosses, the R&D team and workers, frequently showed that the line worker who spends the day making one particular component may identify ways of producing it cheaper, faster and of improved quality.

The above PIN diagram, (Acland, 1995, p. 50), illustrates the above examples by showing how each person will have their positions, usually very different and often highly conflicted, followed by interests and needs which are often initially unknown to the other. It helps to imagine the diagram as being printed on two acetate sheets, one for each person so that they could slide either closer together to form one diagram or moved apart to end up completely separate. If this happens, the two lower sections on interests and needs would no longer show any common ground. Typically in the early stages of a dispute, the sheets have probably moved apart until there is little or no overlap. Commonly this is typically the stage at which disputants decide to seek third party help. By this time conflict and emotions are usually running high, with positions often having reached threats and counter-threats, metaphorically as if each side shouts at the other from the tops of their 'twin peaks'. The key role of the practitioner at this stage – having demonstrated listening with understanding through effective summarising to each – is, through skilled open questioning to 'mine' the two lower potentially 'richer seams' levels, to identify common interests and needs. The effect of such a strategic move is to have the effect of reversing the separation direction momentum and starting to draw the two closer together, increasingly revealing beneficial areas for option development. Often this involves a more creative and optimistic 'give to get' discourse, in which each side can begin to make offers together with requests in 'concession building'. The choice of using these last two words offers a more constructive metaphor than 'compromising' or forced concessions. The LM may need to help start this strategy by inviting each side to propose specific requests and to add what they would be willing to offer in return. The keyword to listen out for here is 'if'. For example, when a person indicates that 'if' they were to consider giving way on 'X', they would want some movement on 'Y' in return, bargaining looks to be possible. The practitioner may now subtly change the *if* to a *when*. For example, summarising that what they are now hearing is that, *when* they start working together on a deal, each side would be looking for reciprocal movement on 'X&Y'. Each disputant can then be asked how feasible that is sounding from where they are sitting, and whether there are any further offers or goals needed. In reality, it is unlikely that this option development process will result in both PIN diagrams ever being completely conjoined. However, what matters most, is how far the two lower levels come to overlap together, especially the lowest zone of fundamental needs. Such a discourse needs to be expanded to consideration of others who might be affected in their nuclear and extended family, community and social networks. A key issue is that mediation with just two or three disputants needs to be envisaged as a 'fishbowl' scene, in which each is backed by many others metaphorically also sitting in the room, and who have strong vested interests in any outcome settlement. Some useful final stage questions on a settlement deal, are to ask what if anything might go wrong, and to consider strategies for what to do if that happens? Some practitioners argue that – having clinched a deal – they are unhappy about 'opening such a can of worms' and risking a breakdown in the deal. However, at that stage, disputants are probably at their most collaborative in the whole process, and so are likely to be ready to agree on plans for any unforeseen glitches. Given what was said above about any vested interests by others, another strategy is to ask who else involved indirectly in the dispute, but not present, may be likely to be supportive of the deal and who might not. If any of the latter are identified, it may be very useful to spend a few minutes considering what they might say or do, in responding to any such challenges and objections. Experienced practitioners will have learned over time that initial 'cutting a deal' outcomes can be vulnerable, and so increasingly became concerned about agreement durability rather than a 'quick-fix'. To conclude this section, two further useful questions should be considered, especially if the process seems to be at an impasse or 'stuckness'. At such a moment a powerful question to ask of all disputants is 'what are each person's worst fears', if a negotiated solution is not found through the mediation process, and what options will they have to consider if that happens.

14 Conclusions

The overriding principle throughout the writing of this book has been to explore and focus on the feasibility of its ideas for would-be untrained dispute resolvers. It has attempted to consider any particular difficulties an LM may encounter in their endeavours, and make suggestions as to how to handle such issues. These key principles have included attempts to make it as safe as possible for LM interventions, and disputants, regarding any risks, pitfalls, key ethical principles, conflicts of interest, legal implications and unforeseen consequences. A respected mediator colleague generally in strong support of this book, nevertheless cautioned that there might be a risk that readers may want to set up in practice as mediators, without undertaking any approved training. This caution merited further reflection yet, arguably, given what was said in the introduction, many people are very good at, and already involved in such everyday problem-solving. They also know how to use many of the fundamental skills of mediation. Consequently, if both of these assumptions are accepted as fair and realistic, they further endorse the reasons for publishing this book. It will hopefully bring beneficial help for such readers with ideas, knowledge, skills, strategies, and principles, hitherto associated with professional dispute resolution.

Readers might find it helpful at this stage to reflect on learning and review initial thinking, as to their inclinations to attempt dispute resolution in their family, community and the work-life world, either for a one-off dispute or as a longer-term lifestyle aspiration. Such a person would need to have the sort of beliefs in themselves and others, that incline them to think the world might just be a better place if more people were attracted to everyday peacemaking opportunities. Starting initially with mainly the family separation and divorce context, mediation has evolved

---

DOI: 10.4324/9781003317005-14

in the UK exponentially over the last three decades and now includes the following practitioner contexts currently endorsed by the College of Mediators.

- Family separation and divorce mediation
- Community (neighbour) mediation
- Civil and commercial disputes mediation
- Peer mediation (young people trained to use mediation in schools to resolve playground disputes)
- Disability conciliation and special educational needs mediation (to resolve disputes around the needs of people with a disability)
- Restorative justice
- Homelessness issues – especially for young people
- Elder mediation

Particularly exciting in that list has been the development of school peer mediation, where selected young people from junior school level upwards are trained to intervene in playground disputes and mediate as co-workers. They are truly amazing and a privilege to watch in practice. Ideally, in time, senior schools will also develop this idea and on into university life. As an evolutionary concept from school children onwards, it augers well for a future of potentially less conflicted society and culture.

Hopefully, the reader will now be in a position to reflect on the overall content of the text – again possibly using a self-assessment rating scale – and consider some of the following questions:

1 To what extent do I now feel more knowledgeable about how disputes affect people's behaviour, and the range of levels involved from everyday irritation, that may perhaps be best ignored, to potential conflict escalation and at worst, risks of serious damage to relationships, or physical harm and legal costs?
2 How far have I been able to understand, internalise and, where necessary realign my values with the fundamental principles described – sometimes known as 'irreducible principles' – without which mediation is at risk of becoming unethical and inappropriate?
3 How far have I understood the skills and strategies that can be selected by the LM from the toolbox? How many are within my everyday ability to use now and which need more development?
4 How different will my involvement in dispute resolution be from now on, compared with any of my previous attempts within the family, neighbourhood or workplace?

Finally, the author wishes the reader every success in their efforts to further develop personal attributes, from what was often hitherto sub-conscious, and their innate abilities to help themselves and others. Such learning and experience have frequently been described by mediation students and trainees of all ages, as 'life-changing', in ways that permeated and enhanced their everyday life.

Recommended further reading

Hopefully, this book will raise thoughts about further related reading and the following list contains some of the author's favourites, all of which have significantly informed his knowledge, practice and writing over some 20 years. Most have also been quoted throughout his books and many published articles. Over several years of designing and running training programmes, it has been noted that some trainers include ever-increasing lists of further reading, but rarely with any comments regarding their particular specific application to learning. These lists often include significantly higher cost texts, that are targeted at the more experienced and advanced stage practitioner, and hence are above the trainee and novice level stages. The following list includes a strong personal preference combination of low cost, high value, easily comprehensible, jargon-free and useful illustrative case examples with application to practice. The publication market in dispute resolution has expanded exponentially and rapidly over the past two decades. Sadly too, so have prices, with new titles, often now being priced at £80–£150, particularly in the higher academic, theoretical and legal practitioner market. For those practising in the 'for profit' sector, that may not be a problem. However, for the trainee, novice and experienced practitioners in the 'not for profit' sector, value for money and price is a big issue. A key recommendation for a buyer is, to consider to what extent does a higher cost book cover anything significantly new or of value-added and application to practice content, than others at a fairer price? As a tip, when considering buying a new book, turn first to the list of chapters, then go to the index. Consider then, to what extent do those lists cover the sort of topics that are helpful in the work. If the list includes topics that the reader either has some knowledge of or is interested in, turn to the pages and sample read to see what if anything is new in there to justify buying. In general, the list is in order of the author's personal favourites, combined with the potential best value for newcomers to the dispute resolution and self-help field.

Social Skills in Interpersonal Communication. Hargie, O., Saunders, C., and Dickson, D. (1994) Third edition. London & New York: Routledge. One of the best and most comprehensive texts on the psychology of interpersonal relationships combined with a logical format that makes it easy to read. By way of added value, it incorporates contemporary research findings and their potential applications in various professional contexts.

Embodied Conflict. The Neural Basis of Conflict and Communication. Hicks, T. (2018). London & New York: Routledge. Coming significantly more up to date in exploring the science of conflict and communication this book digs deeper into the science of the neural workings of the brain. As with the core aims of the main text, it is of value not just to professionally trained conflict specialists but also to anyone struggling to understand the conflicts they face in life. Despite its 'high science' title, the text is presented in layman's terms. Of particular value, and what raises this book above others on the analysis of brain functioning, is how it moves into two key chapters on application to mediation such as Implications for Conflict and its Resolution, and What Can We Do with This information. Applications to Practice.

A Sudden Outbreak of Common Sense. Managing Conflict Through Mediation. Acland, A. (1990). London: Hutchinson Business Books. A valuable early example of the process and writer's analysis of the nine stages of mediation. In keeping with the above text objectives, it seeks to empower non-professionals to prepare to get the best from mediation professionals.

Resolving Disputes Without Going To Court. A Consumer Guide to Alternative Dispute Resolution. Acland, A. (1995). London: Random House. Following on the heels of the above book, this is yet another easy to read book that aims to empower all those caught up in potentially costly disputes to 'escape the legal maze'. Yet again it usefully demystifies the language of legal processes and mediation practice across a range of dispute contexts to enlighten untrained disputants, managers and organisations to make the most of mediation.

Perfect People Skills. All You Need to Get It Right the First Time. Acland, A. (2003). London: Random House Business Books.

To round off this trio of favourite writer's books, this little gem yet again seeks to inform anyone caught up in disputes and conflict as to what people skills are most likely to engage others in constructive settlement negotiations. Expanding on the two previous texts, the writer deals with everyday situations across a range of contexts at home and work, alongside a self-awareness of our behaviour. It follows the essential principles of self-help that were developed throughout the above main book text, especially in its core values regarding people's innate problem solving and core skills capacity.

a-z of mediation. Roberts, M. (2014). Hampshire: Macmillan Publishers. Following the style of the above examples is another small but very comprehensive guide to mediation and dispute resolution. With just over 80 entries the book combines theory, research and practitioner experience to provide a wealth of insight and analysis.

People Skills. How to Assert Yourself, Listen to Others, and Resolve Conflict. Bolton, R. (1986). Australia: Prentice-Hall. A particular favourite very early discovery – is this communication skills handbook jam-packed with excellent knowledge and application examples – including reflective listening; reading body language; assertiveness; three-part assertiveness and handling the push-push back phenomenon – plus lots more all amplifying the above self-help focussed text.

Getting to Yes. Negotiating Agreement Without Giving In. Fisher, R. and Ury, W. (1981). A well-known classic and essential core reading for students of mediation, with a focus on negotiation skills. Once again, it follows the self-help focus and includes useful examples across a range of dispute contexts including family, landlord and tenant, management and unions, to high-level diplomacy. Readers will find the sources of references in the above main book text including more detail on BATNA WATNA, separating people from the problem and using negotiation jujitsu if the other side won't play.

The Language of Negotiation. A Handbook of Practical Strategies For Improving Communication. Mulholland, J. (1991). London: Routledge. Yet more for the student of effective negotiation communication skills and strategies. It includes valuable insights into language and culture; language strategies; spoken interaction; written communication; assertiveness and particular problems. It also helpfully includes useful interactional exercises for the reader to be able to review practice and experience with new skills.

Talk It Out. 4 Steps to Managing People in Your Organisation. Dana, D. (1990). London: Kogan Page. Written by a psychologist this book focuses on disputes in the workplace that can consume up to 25% of the working day which could otherwise be spent on raising company profits. Once again it highlights the self-help ethos and includes aspects on levels of conflict; cultural differences; financial costs of conflict and how to apply its four-step method to turn conflict into cooperation.

References

Acland, A. (1990) *A Sudden Outbreak of Common Sense – Managing Conflict Through Mediation*. London: Hutchinson Business Books.

Berne, E. (2016) *Games People Play: The Psychology of Human Relations*. New York: Grove Press.

Bush, A. and Folger, J. (1994). *The Promise of Mediation. Responding to Conflict Through Empowerment and Recognition*. San Francisco: Jossey-Bass.

Eddy, B. (2007) *Responding to a Hostile Email*. Accessed on 19/09/20. Highconflictinstitute.com/articles/mediation.

Harris, T. (1973) *I'm OK – You're OK*. London: Pan Books.

Haynes, J. and Haynes, G. (1989). *Mediating Divorce. Casebook of Strategies for Successful Family Negotiations*. London: Jossey-Bass.

Irving, H. and Benjamin, M. (2002). *Therapeutic Family Mediation: Helping Families Resolve Conflict*. London: Sage.

Roberts. M. (2008) *Mediation in Family Disputes: Principles of Practice*. Hampshire: Ashgate.

Roberts, M. (2014) *a-z of mediation*. Hampshire: Palgrave Macmillan.

Schneider, C. (2000) *What It Means to Be Sorry. The Power of Apology in Mediation*. Mediation Quarterly 17, 3.

Stultburg, J. (1981) in Roberts, M. (2014) *Mediation in Family Disputes: Principles of Practice*. Farnham Ashgate.

Whatling, T. (2021) *Mediation and Dispute Resolution Contemporary Issus and Developments*. London: Jessica Kingsley Publishers.

Winslade, J. and Monk, G. (2001). *Narrative Mediation: A New Approach to Conflict Resolution*. San Francisco, CA: Jossey Bass.

Index

Note: Page numbers in *italics* denoting figures.

For Product Safety Concerns and Information please contact our EU
representative GPSR@taylorandfrancis.com
Taylor & Francis Verlag GmbH, Kaufingerstraße 24, 80331 München, Germany

www.ingramcontent.com/pod-product-compliance
Ingram Content Group UK Ltd.
Pitfield, Milton Keynes, MK11 3LW, UK
UKHW021456080625
459435UK00012B/527